The Battle of Britain

With the fall of France in June 1940, Britain stood alone against the might of Nazi Germany.

In these pages, the author tells the true story of the R.A.F.'s heroic struggle against the German Luftwaffe, the world's most powerful airforce. He describes in detail the dogfights and the bombing raids, the flimsy aircraft, and the selfless courage of the pilots on whom the fate of Britain hinged. We learn why Britain's radar shield was so successful; how a false invasion alarm set church bells ringing; why the Luftwaffe chief, Hermann Goering, suddenly called off the attack when Fighter Command was on the brink of collapse; and what life was like in Britain during the blitz, with its air raid sirens and its flying bombs.

The book contains more than eighty illustrations, including many diagrams and maps, which help to explain just how much we owe to "the few" who fought in the Battle of Britain.

A British soldier stands
guard by a German
Messerschmitt.

A WAYLAND SENTINEL BOOK

The Battle of Britain

Anthony Hobbs

"Never in the field of human conflict was so much
owed by so many to so few."
(Sir Winston Churchill, 20th August, 1940)

WAYLAND PUBLISHERS LONDON

More Sentinel Books

The Battle of the Atlantic   *Kenneth Allen*
The Story of Gunpowder   *Kenneth Allen*
The Wars of the Roses   *Kenneth Allen*
Cavaliers and Roundheads   *Michael Gibson*
Genghis Khan and the Mongols   *Michael Gibson*
The Samurai of Japan   *Michael Gibson*
China: From Opium Wars to Revolution   *Michael Gibson*
D-Day   *Tudor Edwards*
Nelson's Navy   *Roger Hart*
The Story of the Navy   *Anthony Hobbs*
The Crusades   *Matthew Holden*
Napoleon in Russia   *Matthew Holden*
The Desert Rats   *Matthew Holden*
The Legions of Rome   *Matthew Holden*
War in the Trenches   *Matthew Holden*
A Medieval Siege   *Steven Jeffreys*
Tourney and Joust   *Steven Jeffreys*
The French Foreign Legion   *Nigel Thomas*

SBN 85340 216 7

Copyright © 1973 by Wayland (Publishers) Ltd
49 Lansdowne Place, Hove, East Sussex
Second Impression 1977

Printed in Great Britain by The Garden City Press Limited
Letchworth, Hertfordshire SG6 1JS

Contents

List of Illustrations

1. Britain stands alone

The rise to power in Germany during the 1930s of
Adolf Hitler and the National Socialists, or Nazis,
brought about a revival of German military might
and ambition for conquest.

Adopting a revolutionary form of warfare called
Blitzkrieg, or lightning war, the Germans swept
through Europe's defences with their tanks and
aircraft. They crushed Poland in September, 1939,
to start World War Two. In the following spring,
they overran Norway, Denmark, Holland, Belgium
and France in rapid succession.

British soldiers look back at the Dunkirk beaches from which they have just been evacuated. The European coastline was now completely under German control.

The general pre-war policy towards Hitler's aggression had been one of appeasement. But this had left the Western powers militarily weak and unprepared for the war when it came.

With the fall of France in June, 1940, Britain was the only remaining country who actively opposed Germany. Her position was one of great peril.

She was now menaced by a European coastline completely under German control. Italy had entered the war as Germany's ally; Russia had signed a pact of non-aggression; and the United States, whilst sympathetic towards Britain, remained stubbornly neutral.

Britain herself was woefully unprepared for any kind of war, even for the defence of her own shores. She seemed to the whole world to be at the mercy of the warlord Hitler, and particularly of his bomber aircraft.

Hitler, on his side, confidently expected the British to submit quietly, and sue for peace.

But Mr. Winston Churchill, the British Prime Minister, thought differently. "The Battle of France is over," he declared. "I expect the Battle of Britain is about to begin."

The world at large, however, did not believe that the British nation could survive for long. It was thought her hour of doom had come.

An island in peril

In the early nineteenth century, the French Emperor Napoleon had threatened to send an invasion force across the Channel to Britain. Now, in 1940, the threat of invasion came not only from the sea, but from the air as well.

The British statesman, Stanley Baldwin, had said in 1932: "The bomber will always get through." And ever since then, air attacks had been greatly feared. German bombers had caused appalling destruction and loss of life in their swift raids on European cities. Soldiers on parachutes could also be dropped from the skies.

And how was Britain to defend herself? Since the fall of France, the army was virtually unarmed except for rifles. A large well-armed force, the pick of the British army, had been sent to the Continent early in 1940. But when Belgium and France collapsed so swiftly, British soldiers had to be hastily evacuated from the French port of Dunkirk. Despite heavy attacks from German aircraft, 338,000 British and Allied troops were safely withdrawn. The British army, however, had had to leave behind practically all its heavy equipment, including six hundred tanks. Now there were hardly any guns or tanks with which to defend British soil, and anti-aircraft guns were also in short supply.

During the battles in France and at Dunkirk, the Royal Air Force had lost hundreds of its fighter aircraft and pilots, and it would need time to make good its losses.

The Royal Navy was stronger than the German Navy. But, without adequate air cover, most of the Home Fleet had to retire from the South Coast to a safer anchorage up in Scotland.

The open seas to the west and north of Britain

Above A formation of German Messerschmitts.

Opposite Germany could now attack England from any point along the coast of Europe.

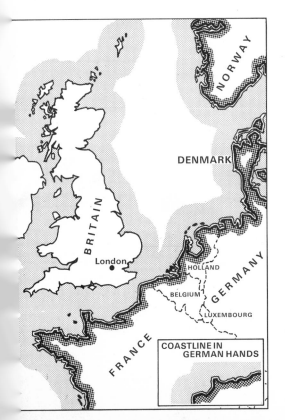

COASTLINE IN GERMAN HANDS

were still controlled by the Royal Navy, but already German submarines, or U-boats, were making raids against merchant shipping. To the east and south, the whole 2,000 mile stretch of European coastline was in German hands.

What would Hitler do? Would he slowly starve Britain by cutting her vital sea arteries by blockade and shipping raids? Would he devastate the island with bombs? Would he send invasion troops?

Hitler had in fact made no plans to deal with continuing British opposition, since he fully expected the British Government to seek a compromise peace very quickly.

He had reckoned, however, without the new fighting spirit of the British as exemplified by their leader Winston Churchill. His war aim was quite simple: "Victory – victory at all costs." There would be no surrender.

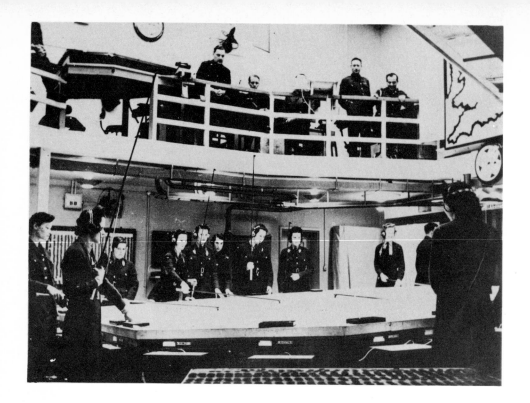

Britain's air defence

Since the main threat now seemed to come from the air, the great question troubling British defence officials was how the country was going to cope with the German air force, which had already played such an important part in the crushing of Europe.

Throughout the 1930s, the British Government's pacification policy had led to a niggardly attitude towards all the country's defences, including the Royal Air Force. This was made worse by the defeatist attitude that said that nothing would be able to stop the bomber.

However, the advent of two new fighter aircraft, the Spitfire and the Hurricane, together with the invention of radar, began to change air defence thinking. People realized that it might now be possible to shoot down the enemy bombers before they had dropped their bombs on target.

Top Operations room at Fighter Command. Notice that all the girls are wearing head-phones. Through these they received up-to-the-minute information about the position of enemy aircraft.

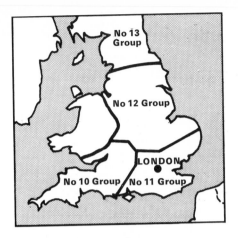

The four geographical groups of Fighter Command.

Airfields and Fighter Command sectors in south-eastern England.

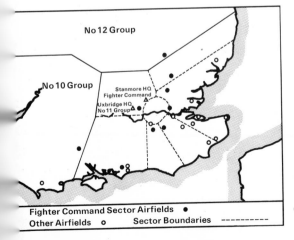

It was therefore decided to set up a special air defence organization. In 1936, Air Chief Marshal Sir Hugh Dowding was made Commander-in-Chief of the new Fighter Command, with headquarters at Stanmore in Middlesex.

Although he was kept short of money and constantly harassed with difficulties, Dowding managed, by 1940, to complete a system capable of defending the nation.

All fighter aircraft came under Dowding's command. He was also responsible for radar stations, anti-aircraft guns, searchlights, barrage balloons and the Royal Observer Corps.

Fighter Command was split up into four geographical groups. The groups, and their commanding officers, were as follows: Group No. 10 (under Air Vice Marshal Christopher Brand) covering central-southern and south-west England; Group No. 11 (under Air Vice Marshal Keith Park), for south-east England; Group No. 12 (under Air Vice Marshal Trafford Leigh-Mallory), for eastern and central England; and Group No. 13 (under Air Vice Marshal R. E. Paul) for the north. In turn, these groups were divided up into smaller areas, or sectors, each one of which contained a main sector station with a number of supporting airfields.

From the moment that radar gave its early warning of approaching enemy aircraft to the time when the fighters were airborne and on their way to intercept, Dowding had built up an unrivalled system of communications and central control.

But the battles in France brought him fresh worries. "If the present rate of wastage continues for another fortnight we shall not have a single Hurricane left in France or in this country," Dowding warned. As it was, 430 fighters were lost. Even more serious was the loss of more than four hundred pilots. By mid-June, the full complement of 1,450 pilots was 360 short.

The victorious Luftwaffe

When Western Europe collapsed, aircraft of the German Air Force, called the Luftwaffe, were able to take up positions on captured airfields facing southern and eastern England. The Luftwaffe had never lost a single battle, and it was the largest and most powerful air force in the world.

The Luftwaffe's Commander-in-Chief, Reich Marshal Hermann Goering, was so confident that he really believed his air force alone could bring Britain to her knees. There were good reasons for his confidence.

By July, 1940, he could boast of a force nearly three thousand strong, including more than 1,300 long-range bombers, 280 dive-bombers, 760 single-engined fighters and 250 twin-engined fighters. This was more than twice the strength of the Royal Air Force.

In 1938 Field Marshal Goering takes the salute at a parade to celebrate the reforming of the Luftwaffe, the German air force.

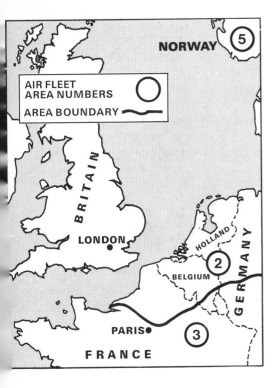

The German Air Fleet areas in Europe, from which air attacks against Britain were launched.

There was also no shortage of trained pilots and crewmen to operate this massive force, which had been hardened and tested in several battles. Even before the start of World War Two, combat technique had been perfected, and men and machines proven, during the Spanish Civil War (1936–1939), when a German air contingent had helped General Franco to gain control of Spain.

For the forthcoming offensive against Britain, the Luftwaffe had two major Air Fleets *(Luftflotten)*, both self-contained forces which operated quite independently of each other.

Air Fleet Two, under Field Marshal Albert Kesselring, had its headquarters in Brussels, and was based on north-east France and the Low Countries. It was responsible for carrying out raids on south-east England. Air Fleet Three, under Field Marshal Hugo von Sperrle, was based on north and north-west France, and was intended to attack England in the south and south-west. Its headquarters were near Paris. Between them, these two air fleets could muster 1,800 serviceable aircraft.

In addition, there was a third but smaller force, Air Fleet Five, which was commanded by General Hans Stumpff and was based in Norway and Denmark. It had 130 long-range bombers and 37 twin-engined fighters.

Altogether, it was an impressive show of air strength. The Luftwaffe, however, was soon to discover serious shortcomings in some of its aircraft, and also in other equipment.

Every attack had to be carefully planned in advance, since aircraft could not be controlled from the ground. Navigation equipment was still primitive and bomb-aimers had to be able visually to sight a target. So the weather, too, was to play an important part in the outcome of the battle, as the victorious Luftwaffe was poised to hurl itself against Britain.

British leaders

WINSTON CHURCHILL From the political wilderness, he became at age 66 the Prime Minister to rally and lead Britain in her "finest hour." Descendant of Duke of Marlborough, he was soldier, war correspondent, statesman, writer, painter. Short, fragile, stumped along on a stick, yet typified bulldog spirit. His supreme asset was mastery over words. Had eternal cigar, gave V for victory sign, sported siren suits. Man of action. Lunched every Tuesday with the King.

AIR CHIEF MARSHAL SIR HUGH DOWDING Built up Fighter Command, which saved Britain. Aged 58, was a stiff, uncompromising character, known as "Stuffy" or that "damned obstinate Scot." Severe to subordinates, merciless to himself. A Spiritualist, was haunted by the problem of survival after death. Sole luxury – collecting gold cuff-links.

AIR VICE MARSHAL KEITH PARK As commander of No. 11 Group, which bore the brunt of the fighting during the battle, was Dowding's first lieutenant and chief tactician. No stranger to a Hurricane, he was one of few officers of air rank who flew combat aircraft. A tall, lean New Zealander, aged 48, thrice decorated in 1914–18 war.

ADOLF HITLER *Führer*, or leader, and founder of Nazi Germany. Magnetic orator, tyrant and demonic visionary. Son of Austrian customs official, dreamed of being an artist before he joined the German army in World War One. Became a corporal, wounded twice and twice decorated for bravery. Formed Nazi Party in 1921, spent nine months in prison, became Chancellor in 1933. Following year, he became dictator, suppressing all opposition. Aged 51.

REICH MARSHAL HERMANN GOERING Vainglorious Luftwaffe chief, Air Minister and Hitler's deputy. Hero of World War One when as a fighter ace he scored 22 victories. Joined Nazi Party in 1921. Now aged 47, pallid monster of 20 stone, drug addict, who could not move without a doctor, valet and nurse. Delighted in fancy uniforms, lived in fairy-tale mansion, played with toy trains. Known as "the Fat One."

FIELD MARSHAL ALBERT KESSELRING Commander of Air Fleet Two, conducting most of the raids against Britain. A former artillery officer, told when he was transferred to the Luftwaffe in 1933: "You are a soldier and have to obey orders." Aged 54.

Two Heinkel III bombers: notice the swastika painted on the tail and the machine-gun mounted in the nose.

2. A test of strength

As his leather-booted troops strutted along the boulevards of Paris, Hitler's thoughts turned to Britain. He was upset by Britain's persistent refusal to make peace. If his terms, which were more than generous in the circumstances, were not accepted, then the country would have to be sternly dealt with. There was only the English Channel – that "canal", as he contemptuously called it – between Britain and the great might of the German army.

On 2nd July, 1940, Hitler ordered a preliminary study to be made of the possibility of invading Britain. Then, on 16th July, he ordered the preparation of such an invasion to go ahead. It was called Operation Sea Lion.

"As England, despite her hopeless military situation, still shows no sign of willingness to come to terms, I have decided to prepare, and if necessary to carry out, a landing operation against her," Hitler told his military chiefs. "The aim of this operation is to eliminate the English motherland as a base from which war against Germany can be continued and, if necessary, to occupy the country completely."

While the invasion preparations were being made, Goering's Luftwaffe could get in some pre-battle practice – a little sparring match with the R.A.F. fighters. Goering, overflowing with confidence, believed that a mere display of Luftwaffe strength would be sufficient to cow the British to such an extent that a German landing would be practically unopposed.

The British reaction to this was summed up by Churchill, who said: "We await undismayed the impending assault."

R.A.F. aircraft

The two Royal Air Force fighter aircraft which won the Battle of Britain were the Spitfire and the Hurricane. They were both single-engined, low-wing monoplanes, and each was armed with eight machine guns. Both these aircraft were developed more through the enterprise of individual designers, with the backing of aircraft companies, than through any Ministry sponsorship.

The Spitfire, a lean, deadly thoroughbred, is acknowledged as one of the classic aircraft of its time, truly an eagle of the skies. But, while superior in performance to the Hurricane, it was not nearly as numerous – at the height of the battle, there were only 370 Spitfires as against 700 Hurricanes.

The Spitfire was designed by Reginald Mitchell, of the Supermarine Company, and was developed from the seaplanes which had triumphed in international air races for the famous Schneider Trophy.

Mitchell, who was dying of tuberculosis, had started the design after becoming alarmed at the rearmament of Germany. Racing against time, Mitchell pressed on and, just before his death in 1937, the first prototype Spitfire was flying. His dream had been realized, but it was a close-run thing – the first operational Spitfires did not appear until June, 1938.

During the forthcoming battle, the Spitfire, which had a top speed of 355 m.p.h., found the German Messerschmitt Bf 109 fighter a worthy antagonist. There was little to choose between them, although the Spitfire was slightly faster and more manoeuvrable.

The Hurricane, mainstay of the front-line squadrons, came from the drawing board of another brilliant designer, Sydney Camm, of Hawker Aircraft Ltd. This robust but slower fighter (with a

Opposite R.A.F. Spitfires, the wings and fuselage camouflaged to break up the plane's outline and make it less easy to hit.

Below The Hurricane fighter, designed by Sydney Camm of Hawker Aircraft.

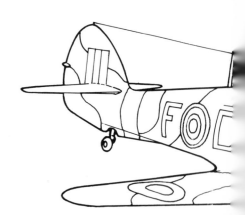

Below The successful Supermarine Spitfire fighter was developed from a seaplane.

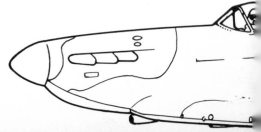

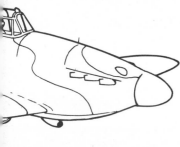

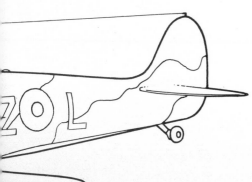

maximum speed of 325 m.p.h.), made its maiden flight in 1935, and was operational by December, 1937.

The German fighter ace, Adolf Galland, found the Hurricanes "very pleasant to shoot down," but Peter Townsend, a Hurricane squadron leader, said: "We ourselves thought the Hurricane was great, and we proved it."

Both the Spitfire and the Hurricane were powered by a single Rolls Royce engine, developing 1,030 horsepower, and were fitted with four American Browning machine guns in each wing. A Browning carried 1,200 rounds, sufficient for fifteen seconds' fire.

Two other fighters, the Defiant and the Blenheim, also played a minor role in the battle. But they were both out-of-date aircraft, and were hopelessly out-classed.

German aircraft

The Luftwaffe's main fighter was the brilliant Bf 109, brainchild of the aeronautical engineer, Professor Willy Messerschmitt. With a top speed of just over 350 m.p.h., it was almost as fast as the Spitfire, but it was not quite so agile, since its controls were difficult to handle at high speeds. It could, however, climb faster and dive faster – two important advantages. It was armed with two machine guns and three 20 mm. cannon which could fire explosive shells.

The Bf 109's greatest drawback was its limited range. Its flying time was only one-and-a-half hours. This meant that it could only fight for a few minutes over Britain before it had to head for home.

The Luftwaffe's other fighter was the Bf 110, also from the Messerschmitt stable. It was known as the *Zerstörer* (the Destroyer), and was Goering's favourite plane. It was a twin-engined aircraft, mounting a powerful battery of four machine guns in the wings, two cannon in the nose and a fifth machine gun, operated by a second crew member, at the rear. But it proved a great disappointment. It was heavy, unwieldy and relatively slow, and soon suffered severe casualties. Eventually, it had to be escorted for its own safety by the Bf 109.

The Germans possessed three main high-level bombers – the Heinkel 111, a slow, medium-bomber;

Above A German Heinkel III bomber. The open flaps show the racks on which the bombs were carried.

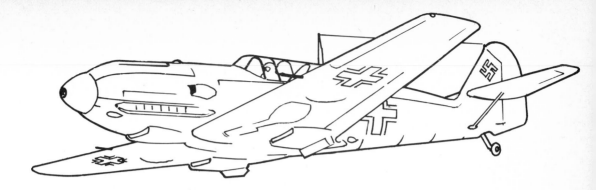

the Dornier 17, known as the "flying pencil"; and
the Junkers 88, the fastest and newest bomber, used
as a "maid-of-all-work." All three were twin-
engined aircraft with ranges, depending on bomb
loads, from 700 to 1,800 miles. It was soon found
that they were too slow and too poorly armed to
beat off British fighters on their own. In addition,
they could not carry sufficient bomb loads to make
really effective mass bombing raids.

Finally, the Luftwaffe had the single-engined
Junkers 87, the Stuka, or dive-bomber, which had
terrorized and devastated the whole of Europe
during the German *Blitzkrieg*. It attacked with great
accuracy in a near vertical dive, at a speed controlled
by dive-brakes and, as it dived, a siren would let out
an ear-splitting shriek. But it was very slow, with
a top speed of only 230 m.p.h., and it received a
tremendous hammering from the R.A.F. fighters.
Eventually, it was withdrawn from the battle.

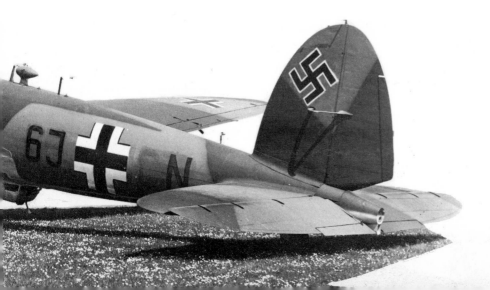

Aircraft production

Having lost 430 fighters in the battles in France and at Dunkirk, R.A.F. Fighter Command was in June, 1940, at a very low ebb. But, by mid-July, the Command had already been built up to its original strength of 650 operational planes, although this figure included nearly a hundred of old types of aircraft.

By mid-summer, production of fighters had increased two-and-a-half times, with a hundred of them leaving the factories every week. In the critical month of September 1940 no fewer than 467 fighters were delivered.

The man mainly responsible for this phenomenal rate of output was Lord Beaverbrook, owner of the Daily Express, who had been appointed Minister of Aircraft Production when Churchill's new government was formed in May 1940. Churchill described Beaverbrook as "a man of altogether exceptional force and genius," while Air Chief Marshal Dowding said: "The effect of his appointment can only be described as magical." Beaverbrook, son of a Canadian Presbyterian minister who had become a millionaire, set factories working at top speed and rode rough-shod over the Air Ministry staff and government civil servants in his bid to produce more fighters. He even appealed to the women of Britain. "Give us your aluminium. We will turn pots and pans into Spitfires and Hurricanes." There was little practical value in this appeal as kitchenware would not yield much high-grade aluminium, but it was good for morale.

Later, he appealed for gold. He also started the Spitfire funds. These funds were very popular as cities, groups and even individuals "bought" a new Spitfire, which was priced at £5,000. In the end, nearly every major town in Britain had its name on a Spitfire. Only a few donors, however, chose to "buy" a Hurricane.

A great deal was also done towards the repair and salvage of wrecked aircraft. By mid-July, the Civilian Repair Organization was returning 160 damaged aircraft a week to operational usefulness; meanwhile, precious parts were being cannibalized from wrecked aircraft on a hundred-acre site near Oxford, known as the "City of Wreckage."

While German industry was capable of producing over a thousand aircraft a month, it concentrated more on bombers than on fighters. This meant that, by the end of the year, Britain had produced 4,283 fighters as against Germany's 3,000.

In May, 1940, Lord Beaverbrook became Minister of Aircraft Production in Churchill's government.

The men who flew

Known as "the few" or "Dowding's Chicks" – both Churchillian expressions – the young, individualistic pilots who flew the Spitfires and Hurricanes became heroic symbols of Britain's defiance.

Their expectation of life was short – more than five hundred were to die and many others were wounded or horribly burned – and the legends which adorned their aircraft, known as crates or kites, expressed their "don't give a damn" attitude. Walt Disney characters, the Saint, Swastikas showering into a chamber pot, became colourful additions to aircraft decoration.

Despite their heavy losses, and the never-ending stream of German aircraft they had to deal with, their

A fighter pilot resting between sorties. His flying helmet is on the arm of the chair beside him.

morale never broke. But, as the battle progressed, they certainly almost reached breaking point. As one pilot said: "We were dead. We were too tired even to get drunk."

The R.A.F. pilots were well-trained. Their weak points were their shooting, and a tendency, especially in the opening stages, to stick to a textbook flying formation.

Volunteer pilots from many countries flew with the R.A.F., in particular pilots from Poland and Czechoslovakia.

Of the battle itself, one pilot, Peter Townsend, said: "The greater issues were beyond us. Our one concern was to boot out the enemy." Another pilot, Richard Hillary, declared: "In a Spitfire, we're back to war as it ought to be – if you can talk about war as it ought to be. Back to individual combat, to self-reliance, total responsibility for one's own fate." Hillary's fate was to be terribly burned.

The German fighter pilots and bomber crews were also highly-trained, and their bombing and shooting was very accurate. At the beginning they were extremely self-confident. But as the battle continued, and the skies were still full of R.A.F. fighters, their morale dropped rapidly. Their morale also suffered because Goering would allow no rest days and no rotation of front-line units. He was also unfairly critical of the fighter pilots, and blamed them for disasters over which they had no control.

As a diversion from the primitive conditions they found on the Channel coast airfields, many German airmen kept pets, including donkeys, hawks, lion cubs and bears. Others took to bathing.

Fighter pilot, Adolf Galland, commented: "We saw one comrade after the other, old and tested brothers in combat, vanish from our ranks. Not a day passed without a place remaining empty at the mess table." It was not an easy life for the pilots on either side.

Radar

Even before the outbreak of World War Two, a series of mysterious brick buildings, surrounded by barbed wire, with 300 ft. tall towers supporting strange looking aerials, began to appear round Britain's south and east coasts. This was Britain's secret weapon, or rather shield – radar, a network of stations which gave Fighter Command the priceless asset of early warning.

From radar, or "radio direction finding" as it was then called, the R.A.F. could detect approaching German aircraft and record their speed, height and approximate numbers. This meant that fighters could then be directed to attack the enemy with a fair degree of accuracy.

A pioneer in the development of radar was Robert Watson-Watt. He had been employed in tracking thunderstorms for the Meteorological Office, when he began to suspect that an aircraft, too, might be detected by the echo set up when it passed through radio waves. Experiments, carried out for the Air Ministry in 1935 by Watson-Watt and a team of scientists, clearly demonstrated that it would be practical to track down aircraft, and the first radar stations began to be built.

Radar is based on the principle that all objects reflect radio waves. If radio waves are beamed into the air, an approaching object, such as an aircraft, will reflect these waves and this reflection or echo can in turn be picked up. It is then possible to determine the direction of the echo, and thus of the aircraft. The distance along that direction may also be determined by timing the journey of the radio waves to the reflecting object and back.

The process is similar to that of a car being driven at night with its headlights on. The radar transmitter,

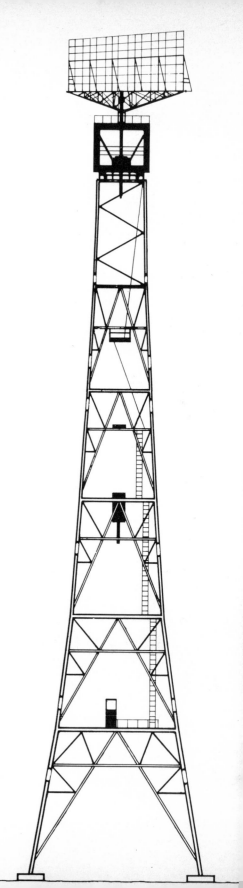

Low-level radar tower as used along the south coast of England.

28

corresponding to the car's headlights, sends out a beam of radio waves. The radar receiver sees nothing until an object comes within range of the radar beam and reflects it – just as the driver sees nothing until an object, reflecting the light, comes into the range of his headlights.

In order for the receiver to pick up the reflected waves, or echoes, transmissions are sent out in short bursts, called pulses. The echoes are then measured on a cathode ray tube, similar to those used in a television set.

The Germans also possessed a form of radar, but only Fighter Command had a system for passing the radar plots, through an elaborate communications network, to the fighter pilot in the air. He could then make use of this information to attack with deadly accuracy.

Above An R.A.F. officer operating radar equipment to help guide an aircraft to base.

Below Plan showing how radar works.

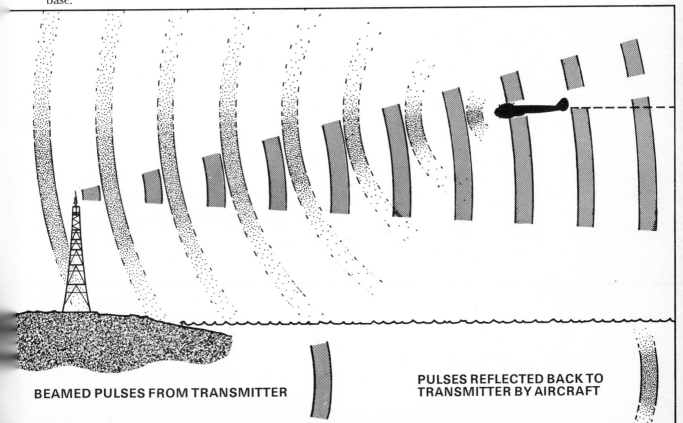

BEAMED PULSES FROM TRANSMITTER

PULSES REFLECTED BACK TO TRANSMITTER BY AIRCRAFT

German intelligence and propaganda

Throughout the Battle of Britain, the Luftwaffe suffered from poor intelligence. This helped to explain, for instance, their failure to recognize the vital importance of Fighter Command's radar screen, and of its well-knit defence organization.

German intelligence chiefs had for some time been puzzled by the groups of tall towers being erected at intervals along the British coast. General Wolfgang Martini, head of Luftwaffe radio intelligence, suspected that the towers related to radar. He therefore persuaded Goering to recommission the *Graf Zeppelin* airship, a gas-filled balloon which had been used during World War One, and to equip her as a flying laboratory. In May and August, 1939, the *Graf Zeppelin* was sent over to spy on the radar masts. Its elaborate equipment, however, failed to work properly and the spying had to be abandoned.

Then, after its European successes, the Luftwaffe seemed to lose interest in Britain's radar. It was not even mentioned in an intelligence report given to Hitler in July, 1940. Neither did the report, called the "Study in Blue" and presented by Luftwaffe Intelligence Chief, Major Joseph Schmid, even mention Fighter Command's widespread communications and control network.

While the report fairly accurately estimated R.A.F. fighter strength as of June 1940, it grossly under-estimated the R.A.F.'s fighter production, allowing for only 180–300 a month, instead of about 450.

This under-estimation of fighter production, coupled with highly over-estimated fighter losses, later led the Luftwaffe chiefs wrongly to assume that Fighter Command must have very few aircraft left.

Radar towers on the cliffs above Dover, 1940. The towers were connected with a beam radio station and radar installations.

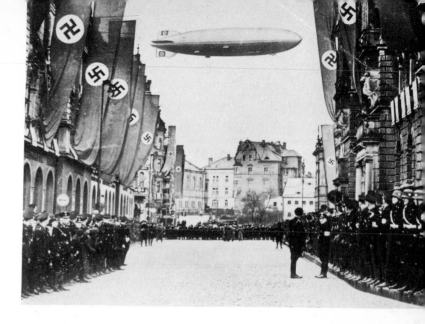

The Luftwaffe also acquired the habit of wiping off the map any R.A.F. airfield they had attacked, regardless of how badly damaged it really was. This meant that the Luftwaffe were always over-confident, and unprepared for the defence they met.

In an attempt to lower the morale of the British people, Germany beamed pessimistic radio broadcasts in English directly at Britain. William Joyce, known as Lord Haw Haw by the British, was to achieve notoriety as one of the commentators. The Germans also established the New British Broadcasting Station, which was supposed to be run by "patriots" somewhere in England, while during the summer three other "underground" stations broadcast for a few minutes each day, giving out the sort of news calculated to undermine morale.

One example of how the Germans tried to make the British public panic was when German bombers scattered empty parachutes, radio transmitters and maps in various parts of Britain. Then the New British Broadcasting Station claimed that German parachutists had landed and were being sheltered by Fifth Columnists (traitors). The lie, however, was soon put to that rumour.

In 1939, the German airship *Graf Zeppelin* (above) was fitted out as a spy ship to examine radar installations on the English coast.

31

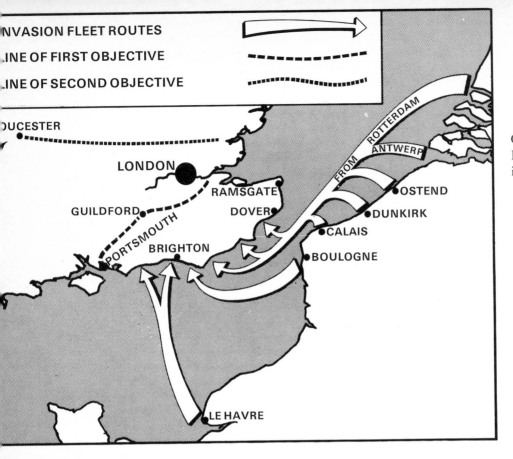

GLOUCESTER

LONDON

RAMSGATE

GUILDFORD   DOVER

PORTSMOUTH

BRIGHTON

BOULOGNE

CALAIS

DUNKIRK

OSTEND

ANTWERP

FROM ROTTERDAM

LE HAVRE

Operation Sea Lion:
Hitler's plan for the
invasion of Britain in 1940

Operation Sea Lion

After Hitler had issued his invasion order of 16th
July, work on Operation Sea Lion went ahead.
The German radio broadcast repeatedly: "People
of Britain, we are coming."

The original plan called for the landing of
thirteen crack infantry divisions, comprising 90,000
troops, along a 200 mile front from Ramsgate in
Kent to Lyme Bay in Dorset. Field Marshal Karl von
Rundstedt would command the operation.

Six divisions embarking from Boulogne and
Calais would land between Ramsgate and Bexhill;
four divisions from the Le Havre area would be put
ashore between Brighton and the Isle of Wight;
while three divisions from the Cherbourg peninsula
would land at Lyme Bay. An airborne division was to

capture the cliff-tops of Dover and Folkestone, while other airborne forces would be dropped at Lyme Bay.

By the third day of the invasion, the Germans hoped to have ashore some 260,000 men, together with 40,000 vehicles, including tanks, to form six panzer and three motorized divisions.

The landing of the first wave of 90,000 men with equipment and supplies called for the assembling of 155 transports, of some 700,000 tons, comprising 1,720 barges, 470 tugs and 1,160 motorboats. Senior German officers thought that the whole operation would be completed within a month, and would be "relatively easy."

German admirals, however, were soon to argue that the 200 mile front was far too wide, that it just was not possible to assemble such a large number of landing craft, and that the invasion fleet would be extremely vulnerable to the British navy and air force. They wanted a much narrower front, stretching just from Folkestone to Eastbourne.

The German generals, in turn, were dismayed at the idea of a narrow front. Fearful of British military strength, one general said: "I might just as well put the troops that have landed through a sausage machine."

A compromise was therefore reached – the invasion would take place between Ramsgate and Brighton.

The German admirals also made it clear that no invasion could be launched until mid-September – they preferred in fact to wait until the following spring. The one essential requirement of the whole operation was air supremacy.

Hitler had no fears on this score. Goering had assured him that the Luftwaffe could clear the skies of R.A.F. fighters within a few days.

General Keitel, on the right, gives Hitler the latest details of the attack on Britain.

Defence preparations

In the meantime, the British had not been idle. Expecting the worst, soldiers and civilians alike had set to, and soon the island was bristling with fortifications, although of a somewhat makeshift nature.

But counter-attacking the enemy after he had landed was only the third line of defence. As Winston Churchill explained, the first line of defence, as always, would be an attack on the enemy's ports, while the second would be the interception and destruction of the invading forces at sea.

However, if the Germans did land, there would be an "entrenched crust" on the likely invasion beaches, "whose defenders should fight where they stood," supported by mobile reserves. Then there

Throughout the Second World War, British beaches looked just like this. Have you ever seen old cement fortifications or barbed wire by the coast?

A member of the Home
Guard Rescue Squad.

would be a line of anti-tank obstacles, manned by the Home Guard, to protect London and the industrial centres. Behind that line would be the main reserves for major counter-attacks.

All beaches now bristled with a variety of defences – mines, barbed wire, barriers, concrete pill-boxes. Machine guns sprouted from piers, bathing was prohibited, sea-front hotels requisitioned.

Further inland, there were anti-tank ditches, pill-boxes and tank-traps, often curious barricades made of old carts, cars and tyres. To prevent air-borne troops from landing, fields, golf courses and parks were scattered with improvized obstacles, including old beds, hayrakes and kitchen ranges.

Military installations, such as airfields, radar stations and fuel depots, were heavily guarded, while thousands of other vulnerable points – bridges, power-stations, vital factories, etc. – also needed protection.

The Home Guard, which was only formed in May, already had 1,500,000 members. These men, many with grey hair and veterans of World War One, looked a motley sight as they drilled on village greens and city parks. Uniforms were few and far between, hats ranged from homburgs to deerstalkers, while weapons included shotguns, pikes, niblicks and even assagais.

The British government was trying hard to prepare the public for the invasion. The Home Office declared: "If Great Britain is invaded, you will receive detailed instructions in good time." The Ministry of Information advised: "Act like a soldier," and "Don't panic."

But, despite all these efforts, Britain's defences were still pitifully weak. The Home Guard had only one rifle for every three men; the army was still in poor shape; there were still far too few guns and tanks.

Channel operations

The preliminary phase of the battle opened in July, 1940, as German air operations gradually developed against British shipping in the Channel, and against the Channel ports. Goering's aim was to gain air supremacy over the Straits of Dover, and to test the strength of Fighter Command by luring out the R.A.F. fighters.

Attacks on shipping began in earnest on 3rd July and, the next day, Portland naval base, near Weymouth, was raided. On 10th July, a convoy off Dover was attacked, but only one ship was sunk.

It all seemed rather unreal to the British public,

A German Heinkel 115 attacks an English ship in the Channel.

who could switch on the radio and hear a live commentary on a fight between Spitfires and Messerschmitts near Dover as if it were a game of football. "Oh! boy . . . I have never seen anything as good as this," enthused the B.B.C. commentator. "The R.A.F. fighters have really got these boys taped . . . no, they have chased them right out to sea . . . there he goes."

But it was a deadly game. On 25th July, sixty bombers attacked a convoy of twenty-one merchant ships, sinking five and damaging another six. The Germans, however, lost sixteen aircraft to the R.A.F.'s seven. Later that day, two British destroyers were dive-bombed by Stukas and one was damaged. Under cover of darkness, German E-boats, fast torpedo boats, sank three of the crippled merchant ships. The Admiralty ordered that no more convoys would sail by day.

Soon afterwards, the Royal Navy lost two destroyers, and a third was badly damaged. Destroyers based at Dover were withdrawn to Portsmouth. It was decided that the next convoy to pass through the Straits of Dover would be better escorted, and would sail at night. Accordingly, twenty-five merchant ships, escorted by barrage balloon vessels and destroyers, slipped through the Straits on the night of 7th August.

Unfortunately, the Germans had erected radar at Wissant, opposite Dover and, early next morning, E-boats attacked, sinking three ships and damaging two more. Later, two waves of Stukas, eighty at a time, with numerous escorts, and more E-boats, attacked the stricken ships.

Seven squadrons of Spitfires and Hurricanes were scrambled and, in a furious scrap, brought down thirty-one German planes for the loss of only nineteen. But seven ships had been lost and many more damaged.

3. Destroy the R.A.F.!

This preliminary skirmishing had cost the Germans nearly three hundred aircraft, a high price to pay, although they had managed to sink eighteen merchant ships and four destroyers. Fighter Command, wisely conserving its resources by committing its fighters in small numbers only, had lost just 148 planes.

"The R.A.F. must be destroyed!" Hitler thundered. Without supremacy in the air, Germany could never launch an invasion force.

On 1st August, Hitler directed: "In order to establish the conditions necessary for the final conquest of England, I intend to continue the air and naval war against the English homeland more intensively than before." And he ordered the Luftwaffe to "overcome the British air force by all means at its disposal, and as soon as possible."

Goering was still in no great hurry: invasion preparations would take some time, and the weather was unfavourable for attack. In any case, he was confident that R.A.F. fighter defences in southern England could be destroyed in four days. To smash the R.A.F. completely would take a little longer – perhaps two to four weeks.

At Karinhall, his palatial mansion near Berlin, the capital of Germany, Goering relaxed amidst the silk and silver hangings, the crystal chandeliers, and the canary cages shaped like dive-bombers. In between stag hunting, playing with toy trains, and admiring his collection of paintings and diamonds, he began to plan the great onslaught that would bring Britain to her knees.

Goering, the German commander responsible for the air attack on Britain, relaxes with his pipe. He is wearing the German Iron Cross around his neck.

Goering and his two Air Fleet commanders, Kesselring and Sperrle, decided that the big day, to be called *Adlertag* (Eagle Day), would start on 10th August. The weather was still bad, however, and Eagle Day was later postponed until 13th August.

Attack on radar stations

Before beginning the all-out assault on Fighter Command, Goering ordered that the opposition should be softened up a little and an attempt made to knock out some of the radar stations. The attacks would take place on 12th August, the opening of the British grouse season.

Early that morning, radar plotters at their stations in southern England began picking up on their screens the V-shaped blips of light that meant the approach of enemy aircraft from across the Channel.

The plotters, mostly members of the Women's Auxiliary Air Force, went on reporting the positions of the aircraft until the raiders were directly over-head. One woman realized what was happening, and cried, "My God, they're bombing us."

Six stations between Dover and the Isle of Wight came under heavy dive-bomb and low-level attacks. Four stations were damaged, but were back on the air within a few hours. Fifteen bombs, however, had landed right on the Isle of Wight Ventnor station, and it was put out of action for nearly two weeks. But the Germans never knew they had forced a breach in Fighter Command's defences. Pulses continued to be sent out from another transmitter just as if Ventnor was still working.

German bombers also raided the vulnerable airfields of Manston, Lympne and Hawkinge on the Kent coast. At Hawkinge, hangars and workshops were smashed and the runway pitted. Manston was even more severely damaged, and operations there were suspended for a time.

Later in the day, the Luftwaffe attacked two convoys in the Thames Estuary. Stukas also made a

Above An Observer Corps outlook post. The observers detected and plotted the height and course of all aircraft passing overhead and relayed the information back to the Control Centre.

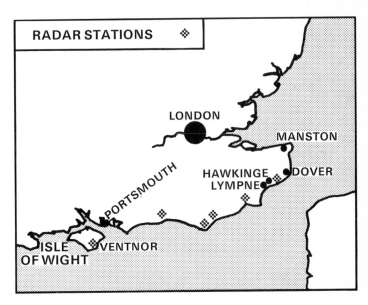

RADAR STATIONS

LONDON

MANSTON

PORTSMOUTH

HAWKINGE
LYMPNE

DOVER

ISLE
OF WIGHT

VENTNOR

Above right The airfields and radar stations in the southeast of England attacked by the Germans on 12th August.

raid on Portsmouth dockyard, where tempting naval targets lay helplessly at anchor, but they succeeded only in hitting a brewery.

In twenty or more scraps during the day, Spitfires and Hurricanes shot down a total of thirty-two German aircraft, but twenty-two R.A.F. fighters were lost as well.

It was at this stage that Goering made the first of his many tactical errors during the battle. He believed that it was pointless to continue these attacks on radar stations, "since not one of those attacked has been put out of action." He considered it would take weeks of saturation bombing before any vital equipment was damaged, and so he called off the attacks.

He did not realize how much damage had already been caused, nor that the radar stations, with their operations rooms above ground, were in fact extremely vulnerable to air attack.

41

Eagle Day

When at last the opening day of the grand assault arrived, it was something of an anti-climax. Cloud and mist appeared over the Channel on the morning of 13th August, and Goering decided to postpone the offensive until the afternoon. However, because of faulty communications, not all the postponement orders got through in time.

This caused a great deal of confusion. Some bomber formations were taking off without fighter escorts, and some fighters were leaving without any bombers to escort.

Although a Messerschmitt fighter tried to warn

them by waggling its wings at them, a whole group of eighty Dorniers, led by Commodore Johannes Fink from Air Fleet Two, flew across the Channel without any fighter cover. The low clouds gave the bombers protection from probing R.A.F. fighters, and a break in the clouds right over the target allowed the Dorniers to unleash their lethal loads directly onto Eastchurch in Kent, destroying five Blenheim aircraft on the ground. This was fine, except that Eastchurch was a Coastal and not a Fighter Command airfield, and, on their way home, the Germans were intercepted and four Dorniers were shot down in flames by Spitfires and Hurricanes. Fink was not in a very good humour when he landed.

Simultaneous attacks over Sussex by bombers from Air Fleet Three were all intercepted and driven off. Then a group of Messerschmitt Bf 110s arrived off Portland without the bombers they were meant to accompany. No fewer than five were shot down before the rest turned tail.

The main attacks came in the afternoon, although the weather was still cloudy. Forty well-escorted bombers from Sperrle's Air Fleet Three crossed over the Hampshire coast and, despite heavy anti-aircraft fire, bombed Southampton, causing fires to break out in the docks.

To the east, in Kent, fifty bombers from Kesselring's Air Fleet Two, also heavily-escorted, attacked Detling, another Coastal Command station. Many airmen were taking tea in the canteen when the first bombs fell. More than fifty people, including the station commander, were killed; many aircraft were destroyed, and hangars and other buildings were smashed.

The Luftwaffe was already congratulating itself on a victory, claiming to have destroyed at least eighty R.A.F. fighters. In fact, after flying 1,485 sorties, the Germans had destroyed only thirteen fighters and had themselves lost forty-five aircraft.

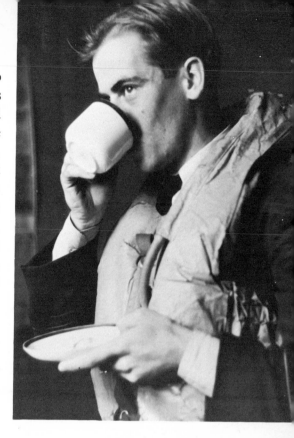

The scene at a Fighter Command station, as a pilot relaxes between sorties. Round his neck he is wearing a Mae West, an inflatable life jacket for use if his plane crashes into the sea.

Opposite Eagle Day – the day for the all-out German attack on Britain was ruined by bad weather. You can see this plane's reflection in the water lying on the runway.

43

"Black Thursday"

After a day of bad weather, Thursday, 15th August was intended to be the Luftwaffe's "big throw." All three air fleets were ordered to carry out massive raids. The German radio boasted: "John Bull will be smoked out. Either he will surrender or England will be annihilated." But 15th August was doomed to go down in Luftwaffe history as "Black Thursday," the worst beating it had taken so far.

The venture into the fray for the first time of Air Fleet Five, based in Norway and Denmark, proved completely disastrous. It lost a massive total of twenty-three aircraft and was never to take part in the battle again.

Altogether, after flying no fewer than 1,780 sorties, the Luftwaffe lost seventy-five aircraft. The R.A.F. had thirty-two fighters destroyed.

While the other two air fleets were hammering the south, Air Fleet Five sent two formations across the North Sea to attack north-east England, in the belief that most of the R.A.F. fighters had been transferred from there to the south. They found, however, to their cost, that the switch had only been between tired and rested squadrons, and that the R.A.F. was still at full strength in the north.

Right A German Dornier aircraft, shot down by British fighters, dives in flames to the sea.

44

German aircraft flying in
formation across the
Channel on a daylight
bombing raid.

The first formation of sixty-five Heinkels, escorted
by thirty-five Messerschmitt Bf 110s, was picked up
by radar when it was still far out at sea. This gave
No. 13 Group plenty of time to scramble five
squadrons. Spitfires dived down on the enemy, who
were blinded by the sun, and hacked their formations
to pieces. In a series of other engagements, the Germans lost a total of eight Heinkels and seven Bf 110s.

The second formation of fifty unescorted Junkers
88 bombers were intercepted by three squadrons
from No. 12 Group. Although eight of their number
were shot down, the rest managed to get through to
the R.A.F. bomber base of Great Driffield in York-
shire, where they destroyed ten bombers on the
ground.

In the south, the British defence was less successful:
the vast number of Luftwaffe raids confused the
radar picture, and R.A.F. fighters had to chase
backwards and forwards, looking for their prey.

Forty Stukas, escorted by sixty fighters, attacked
the Kent airfields of Lympne, Manston and Hawkinge, and Lympne was severely damaged. The
Short aircraft factory at Rochester was badly hit,
and another fighter station at Martlesham Heath in
Suffolk was raided.

That evening bombs were dropped on West
Malling in Kent, and also on Croydon, where a
hangar containing fifty training aircraft burst into
flames and eighty people were killed or injured.

Fighter tactics

In the early stages of the battle, R.A.F. fighter pilots flew in rigid formation, as they had been taught during their training. A squadron of twelve aircraft would fly in four sections of three in tight V-shaped "vics," which the Luftwaffe nicknamed "the bunch of bananas."

This meant that pilots had to concentrate on maintaining their position with wing-tip five feet from wing-tip, instead of keeping a look-out for enemy planes.

Some squadron commanders soon put aside the training manual, and taught their pilots to fight in pairs, in three sections of four. Sometimes "weavers" were provided, who flew to and fro to protect "tail end Charlie," as the last man in the squadron was called.

Johnnie Johnson, the top-scoring British fighter ace who notched up thirty-eight victories in World War Two, complained: "We searched desperately for someone to tell us what to do and what not to do, because this, we fully realized, would shortly mean the difference between life and death."

At first British fighters were sent up in single squadrons. Later they flew in pairs, with Spitfires tackling the German fighters, while Hurricanes attacked the bombers. Towards the end of the battle, as many as five squadrons, over sixty fighters, would fly in a single wing. But, once the enemy was sighted and the cry of "tally-ho" had gone up, it was each pilot for himself in a series of individual encounters, or "dog-fights."

The Hurricane, outclassed by the Messerschmitt Bf 109, avoided destruction by flying in a tight circle, which the larger German aircraft could not follow. Polish pilots, on the other hand, loved the

46

Four groups of Spitfires flying in "vic" formation.

German Messerschmitt Bf 110s fly in a defensive "circle of death," as an English Spitfire (in the centre) comes to attack them.

head-on attack, which required great nerve since the combined closing speed would be about 600 m.p.h., and also a quick pull-out if they were to avoid collision.

Gaining height over one's opponent was always an advantage, and a pilot liked to attack with the sun at his back, so that the enemy was blinded by it.

The German fighter pilots flew in *Schwärme*, or groups of four, consisting of two pairs, with the leader navigating and the wingman keeping a lookout. *Schwärmer* flew at different heights, so that the starboard or right-hand group could search into the sun, and guard the others.

The Messerschmitt Bf 110s often adopted a defensive tactic called the "circle of death." This meant that they would fly in a tight circle, each one guarding the other one's tail.

Below A squadron of R.A.F. Spitfires flying off on a reconnaissance mission.

Air/sea rescue

Although it was over the British Channel coast that the battle was raging, an R.A.F. pilot who came down in the sea stood less chance of being rescued than did his German counterpart. Survival for the R.A.F. was largely a question of luck.

At the beginning of the battle, the British air/sea rescue service was extremely haphazard. Only eighteen rescue launches had been provided to cover Britain's entire coastline, spotter planes were few and far between, and no dinghies were issued to the pilots, who had to make do with lifejackets.

During the last three weeks of July, 1940, well over two hundred R.A.F. aircrew were reported killed or missing over the sea.

Opposite Pilots of a German bomber squadron inspect their gear before a raid on England. Do you see the parachutes strapped onto their backs?

Below A British aircrew clambers to safety aboard an inflatable rubber dinghy. You can see how the Mae West around the neck of the man at the back is helping to keep him above water.

Some were lucky, incredibly lucky. Flying Officer Paul Le Rougetel had been shot down and was still drifting as night fell. He was just about to collapse when his luminous wrist-watch was spotted by the coxswain of Margate lifeboat, and he was brought to safety. The Margate lifeboat also came to the rescue when Richard Hillary was shot down. He was terribly burned, and had been floating for many hours in his life-jacket when they found him.

Flying Officer Geoffrey Page had baled out when his aircraft was shot down in flames. He remembered later noticing strips of flesh from his burned hands and face floating in the water. He was picked up by a motor-boat just in time. Another pilot was rescued by a young girl in a fragile canoe.

Flying Officer Russell Aitkin was appalled by these losses. Very soon, he had borrowed a float-plane and had set up a private rescue service off the Isle of Wight.

It was not until the end of August, however, that the rescue service showed official signs of improvement. Then a joint-Services rescue organization was set up, with R.A.F. launches and naval patrol craft, R.A.F. spotter planes, and twelve Army aircraft to drop dinghies.

The Germans, by contrast, had a much more efficient service, which used numerous fast sea launches and thirty Heinkel sea-planes. Later, they also introduced sea rescue floats, nicknamed "lobster-pots", which were permanently stationed in the middle of the Channel. These floats contained first-aid supplies, dry clothes, food, a radio and even sometimes a game of draughts.

In addition, German air crews were normally equipped with inflatable rubber dinghies, life-jackets and also survival kits, which contained a Very pistol, some food and brandy, and a chemical which would make a bright green stain in the water so that they could be easily recognized.

A British scene

So far in the battle, German air attacks had been mainly directed against military installations, and had done little to change the British people's way of life. On a clear day, civilians could watch these aerial dog-fights; the vapour trails discharged by the aircraft formed intricate patterns in the sky, like an abstract oil painting.

Occasionally there was excitement, when a plane crashed for example, or a pilot baled out. Home Guards with rifles and farmers waving pitchforks would rush to the scene. Once he had been identified, an R.A.F. pilot would often be regaled with food and drink, or asked for his autograph.

Sometimes the horror of war was brought home to civilians, when an aircraft crashed onto a house or farm, causing its toll of death and destruction.

It had been an early summer and the weather generally continued warm and sunny. The cuckoo was reported late in arriving. Other birds, however, were differently affected by the air battle. Chickens were said to give a loud cackling before the sirens sounded the alarm; pheasants, too, gave early warning. But swallows and swifts seemed totally unconcerned by the aircraft fighting around them.

The increased taxation on spirits, beer and tobacco was much more a subject of general conversation than German raiders. The introduction of food rationing, with restrictions on sugar, bacon, tea and butter, also caused grumbling. In Kent, farmers were concerned about the heavy wheat crop, and the glut of strawberries.

Pubs were doing a roaring trade and cinemas were well-attended – "Gone With The Wind" was a big box office success. Bowls and cricket were still being played on village greens; and newsvendors

50

Children sheltering in a trench during an air-raid in Kent.

Vapour trails left by aircraft
fighting over London on
6th September, 1940.

gave the aerial contests a sporting flavour by reporting the aircraft losses in the same way as cricket scores.

Generally, people went about their normal business, despite all the signs of impending danger. In the cities, landmarks were now hidden behind sandbags, while buses and trams ran without destination boards. The skies were filled with barrage balloons.

Travelling, particularly at night, was hazardous. Signposts and street names had been taken down, lights were blacked out and railway station signs removed. On parking, motorists were obliged to immobilize their cars.

Every day, hundreds of gas masks, from the millions which had been distributed in case the Germans resorted to gas warfare, were left behind in public transport.

Rumours spoke of spies and parachutists. And the church bells were silent. They would only be rung again to give the alarm in case of invasion.

Goering maintains the pressure

The Germans believed that the R.A.F. was already facing defeat. Their faulty intelligence calculated that the R.A.F. only had three hundred serviceable fighters left, since 770 aircraft had been destroyed or lost through wastage. In fact, however, Fighter Command still had six hundred operational aircraft, with another 235 ready to join.

The Luftwaffe offensive continued on 16th August, with more than 1,700 sorties flown in raids mainly against airfields. West Malling in Kent was hammered when seventy escorted bombers managed to break through the British fighter screen. The sector station of Tangmere, near Chichester, was also blasted.

Pilots, their aircraft short of fuel, faced the nightmare situation of having to land at Tangmere while the airfield was still being dive-bombed. Buildings

were wrecked, electricity and water supplies cut off, and fourteen aircraft were destroyed or damaged.

After the raid, Tangmere's 601 Squadron exacted revenge. They shot seven of the bombers to pieces, and forced many more to limp home, badly damaged.

During the action, the Hurricane of Pilot Officer Billy Fiske, an American volunteer, was hit. He managed to land, but his aircraft was then shot up by German fighters. Ground crew dragged Fiske from the burning wreckage but he died soon after of his burns. There is a plaque to commemorate him in St. Paul's Cathedral. It reads: "An American citizen who died that England might live."

Other raids followed. Forty-six training aircraft were destroyed at Brize Norton, but this had little effect on the battle.

The following day was quiet, but the Luftwaffe renewed attacks on 18th August. The Kent airfields of Kenley, Biggin Hill, Croydon and West Malling were attacked, and Kenley was severely damaged.

More raids took place over Hampshire, West Sussex and the Thames Estuary, but the Germans met here with fierce opposition. A formation of Stukas in particular was severely mauled – eighteen out of twenty-eight were shot down or damaged. The day ended with the Luftwaffe having lost seventy-one aircraft, as against the R.A.F.'s twenty-seven.

The four days that Goering had allowed in his calculations to gain air supremacy over southern England were over, and there was still plenty of fight left in the R.A.F.

Winston Churchill summed it up when he said: "Never in the field of human conflict was so much owed by so many to so few."

Refuelling a Spitfire at a Fighter Command station in Kent. The most important thing, at the height of the Battle of Britain, was to keep as many planes in the air as possible.

4. London's burning

Bad weather brought the German air offensive to a
halt, and the next five days of rain and cloud gave
Fighter Command a well-deserved rest. Air Chief
Marshal Dowding counted up his losses. Between
8th and 18th August, 183 fighters had been shot down,
with another thirty destroyed on the ground. What
was worse, ninety-four pilots had been killed, and
another sixty wounded.

On the other side of the Channel, Hermann
Goering was doing similar calculations and, as a
result, decided to bring in some changes. The Stuka,
which had taken a fearful beating, was to be withdrawn from the battle. But Goering could not bring
himself to withdraw the Messerschmitt Bf 110, which
had also been severely mauled. Instead, his favourite
Zerstörer was in future to be escorted by the Bf 109.

Alarmed by high bomber losses, Goering ordered
the Bf 109s to stay closer to their bomber charges.
This was a catastrophic misuse of a brilliant fighter,
but Goering blamed the actions of the Bf 109 pilots
for these heavy losses.

The main concentration of German attack would
from now on be directed against south-east England.
To this end, every single Bf 109 was taken from
Sperrle's Air Fleet Three and transferred to Kesselring's Air Fleet Two.

Goering told his air fleet commanders: "We have
reached the decisive period of the air war against
England. The vital task is the defeat of the enemy air
force. Our first aim is to destroy the enemy's fighters."

But, on the very day that the Luftwaffe resumed
its attacks, bombs were accidentally dropped on
London – a mistake which was to change the whole
course of the battle, and lead eventually to a British
victory.

R.A.F. Spitfires drawn
up on a Kent airfield.
During the ten days
between 8th and 18th
August, 1940, Fighter
Command lost 213 fighter
aircraft.

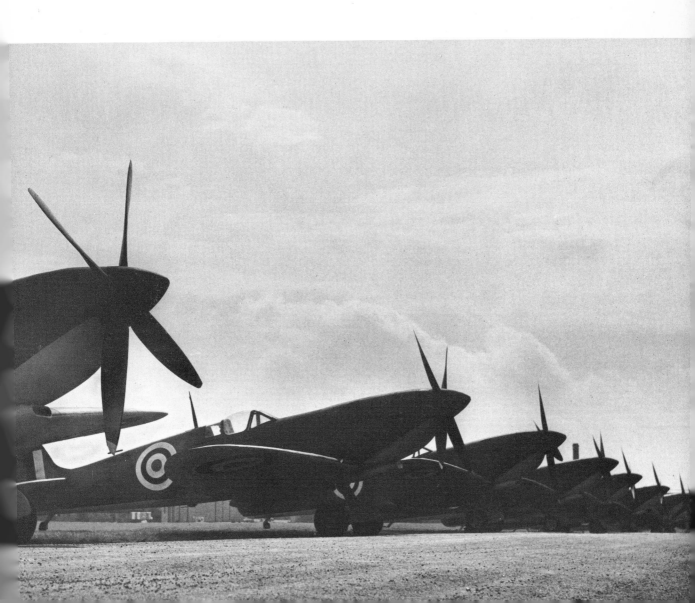

A question of bombing

When, on 24th August, the weather improved, Goering launched his second bid for air superiority. Soon the air raid sirens were sounding again all over southern England.

Air Fleet Two adopted new tactics, in a series of well-directed raids. Some aircraft remained airborne on the French side of the Channel. This meant that Air Vice Marshal Park's No. 11 Group were kept guessing, since radar could not tell the difference between bombers and fighters, nor tell when the aircraft would suddenly dash across the Channel.

And, once the mass formations had passed through the radar screen, they would split up into small

Opposite The mess and confusion in a London street after a German air-raid. The puddles show how much water the firemen have had to use to put out the fires.

Below In September 1940, the Germans bombed London docks. Here you can see the thick, dark smoke rising from the burning buildings.

raiding parties. In addition, the increased number of German fighters meant that the R.A.F. had difficulty in piercing the German escort screen. This, in turn, meant that the bombers had a better chance of reaching their targets.

Heavy attacks were made on the sector stations of North Weald and Hornchurch, and they were only saved by strong anti-aircraft fire. Manston was less fortunate; it was so badly damaged that it had to be completely abandoned.

Meanwhile Air Fleet Three managed to scrape up sufficient escorts and raided Portsmouth dockyard. There, the heavy concentration of anti-aircraft fire led to the bombers scattering their bombs all over the city.

Goering had ordered round-the-clock bombing. That night, 170 bombers flew over Britain. Some of them were detailed to attack the Thameshaven oil refinery and an aircraft factory at Rochester, but they lost their way and let their bombs fall on London, destroying houses and killing civilians in the East End.

Thinking that the attack was deliberate, the British reacted swiftly. The following night, eighty R.A.F. bombers flew across to Germany with orders to bomb Berlin. It was a cloudy night, and many of the bombers lost their way, but twenty did manage to drop their loads on the German capital.

Hitler and the Berliners were furious. Three more times in the next ten nights, R.A.F. bombers scattered bombs over Berlin. German newspaper headlines screamed: "Cowardly British Attack" and "British air pirates over Berlin."

An incensed Hitler shouted: "When the British declare they will increase their attacks on our cities, then we will raze their cities to the ground. We will stop the handiwork of these night air pirates, so help us God."

Fighter Command
at last gasp

Meanwhile, the Germans continued their relentless pounding of Fighter Command. By early September, it was close to breaking point. The R.A.F. pilots were physically and mentally worn out. Airfields were being left in smoking ruins, with runways pitted with craters and unexploded bombs, buildings levelled to the ground and electricity, gas and water supplies cut off. The whole network of control and communications was collapsing.

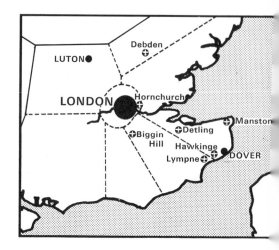

Repair teams worked night and day to keep the fighter stations operating. Somehow, the battered squadrons continued the fight.

The last two days of August saw the fiercest forty-eight hours of fighting in the entire battle. The Luftwaffe made a supreme effort to finish off the remaining British fighters, and destroy the vital sector stations. Blackest day of all was 31st August, when the R.A.F. lost thirty-nine fighters to the Luftwaffe's forty-one. Altogether, a total of sixty-five British fighters were destroyed in those two terrible days.

The Kent airfields of Biggin Hill, Manston, Hawkinge, Lympne and Detling were all shattered on 30th August. Luton, too, was attacked. Fifty barrage balloons were shot down in flames over Dover, which signalled the start of fresh raids the following day, when Hornchurch, Biggin Hill and Debden were badly punished.

Then the Luftwaffe varied their tactics by attacking aircraft factories. Vickers-Armstrong at Brooklands was bombed on 4th September, and eighty people killed. Now fighters had to be detailed to protect the factories producing the vital aircraft.

Fighter Command was at its last gasp. Of No. 11 Group's seven sector stations, six were seriously

Left The Luftwaffe's targets on 31st August, the blackest day for the R.A.F. in the whole of the Battle of Britain.

Below The alert has sounded – R.A.F. aircrew rush to their Hurricanes. Look for the Mae Wests round their necks, and the parachutes on their backs.

damaged and another five airfields were in bad shape. During the past two weeks, Fighter Command had lost 295 fighters with another 170 damaged, while 103 pilots were killed and 128 wounded. The experienced pilots were now either dead or exhausted; the new men were still raw, and too few in number.

As Air Vice Marshal Park said: "Had the enemy continued his heavy attacks against Biggin Hill and the adjacent sectors ... the fighter defences of London would have been in a perilous state."

But, on 2nd September, 1940, Hitler had ordered "reprisal raids." The following day, Goering directed the Luftwaffe to attack London. This fatal decision, although it led to much suffering in London itself, was to save Fighter Command from destruction. It was Goering's second blunder.

Biggin Hill

One of the worst-hit fighter stations during this period was Biggin Hill, a 450-acre hilltop site in Kent known as "Biggin-on-the-Bump." It was one of No. 11 Group's essential sector stations in guiding fighter squadrons to intercept intruders, and was raided eight times during the battle, including five consecutive attacks in three days.

It was left a smoking shambles, with every building flattened, so that it could barely operate even one of its three squadrons.

The bombers came three times on 30th August; the third raid in the early evening nearly obliterated the station. While a dozen Messerschmitt Bf 109s strafed with machine guns and cannon, nine Junkers 88 aircraft made a fast low run over the airfield and, with devastating accuracy, dropped two bombs each, all right on target. Workshops, barracks and other

buildings were blown to bits, two aircraft on the
ground were burned out, and all electricity, gas and
water supplies cut off. Thirty-nine personnel, mostly
W.A.A.F.s, were killed, and another twenty-six
injured.

By noon the following day, a works party from the
local post office had repaired the main electric cable,
which had been cut in three places, and other
temporary repairs had also been carried out. But, in
the early evening, the raiders were back again,
knocking down everything that had just been put up.

Two squadrons were hastily scrambled as twenty
German Dorniers approached. W.A.A.F. plotters
and telephone operators in the operations room
continued to plot the intruders as the first bombs
fell. With telephone lines cut, the W.A.A.F.s took
what cover they could, with the exception of
Sergeant Helen Turner and Corporal Elspeth
Henderson, who stuck to their posts to man one uncut
line. Then a 500 lb bomb scored a direct hit on the
operations room and, from amongst the broken
glass, plaster and twisted metal, the two women
were dragged out still alive.

Corporal Henderson calmly commented to her
commanding officer: "I joined the W.A.A.F.s to see
a bit of life." Both she and Sergent Turner were to
receive the Military Medal for their bravery.
Surprisingly, only one person was killed in that raid,
a boy bugler who had volunteered to help the
signals staff.

As the dead were being buried on Sunday, 1st
September, the operations room, now housed in the
village butcher's shop, scrambled the one remaining
squadron in an attempt to drive off yet another raid.

An air-base commander
(notice his flat cap, and the
gold on its peak) snatches a
moment's rest before the
alert goes for the next
German attack.

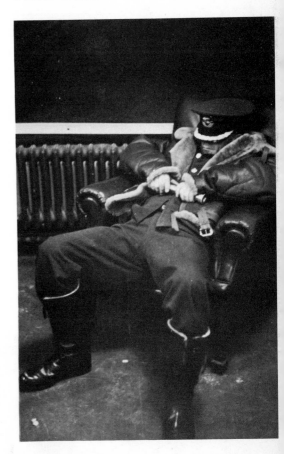

61

Air armada

Nothing like it had ever been seen before. On the afternoon of 7th September, the sky was blackened with aircraft, as three hundred bombers and six hundred fighters amassed in two huge waves over France. The bombers, with thick clusters of escorts, were in close-knit formations, flying in layers between 14,000 and 20,000 feet. More fighters swarmed around them at heights of up to 30,000 feet.

This massive air armada, twenty miles wide, was on its way across the Channel to attack the "biggest target in the world" – London. Hermann Goering, resplendent in white uniform and pink leather boots, had travelled to watch them in his luxurious personal train, and now stood proudly on the clifftops at Cap Gris Nez. Soon London would be bombed into submission.

British radar quickly picked up this huge invading force, and twenty-one squadrons, every available Spitfire and Hurricane, were rapidly scrambled. But No. 11 Group Headquarters (Park was unavoidably absent that day) was not expecting a raid on London, and the fighters were sent to protect aircraft factories and sector stations.

With many of the fighters in defensive positions north of the Thames, the way to London was clear. Remorselessly the bombers, now without the escorting Bf 109s which had reached the limit of their range, droned over Sevenoaks and on to London where, in formation after formation, they dropped 300 tons of high explosive bombs, mainly on the docks and the East End. Soon, hundreds of fires were raging. Row upon row of old houses were collapsing like a pack of cards.

An area a mile-and-a-half square, between North Woolwich Road and the Thames, was razed to the

Opposite The raid is over but the destruction remains. Smoke rises from the ruins of a London building, and pipes and sewers lie on the surface, forced out of the ground by the explosion.

A rescue squad frees a woman trapped in the remains of a house which was hit by a German bomb.

ground; at Silvertown, people cut off by the raging fires had to be rescued by barge and tug. Three hundred civilians were to die, and another 1,300 were seriously injured.

The frustrated R.A.F. fighters managed to make some amends when the Germans headed for home. The Poles of No. 303 Squadron, in particular, attacked with great ferocity. Nearly every pilot got his bomber, and ten Dorniers were shot down. "We gave them all we'd got," said Squadron Leader R. G. Kellett, their British commander. But the damage had been done.

"For the first time we have struck at England's heart," gloated Goering. "This is an historic hour."

That night, Goering sent over a further 250 bombers which, guided by the fires still blazing in London, succeeded in dropping another 300 tons of bombs, and thousands of incendiary bombs, within a ten-mile radius of Charing Cross.

Invasion imminent

In the meantime, the Germans had been busy preparing another kind of armada – a fleet of boats, to transport the invasion force across the Channel. Along the canals and rivers of Europe, hundreds of barges, tugs and motor vessels hurried to join the deep-sea transport ships at ports in France, Belgium and Holland.

Already, the 90,000 troops which would spearhead the assault on the British beaches were waiting at their ports of embarkation. The Stukas, previously withdrawn from the air battle, were reappearing opposite Dover, while bombers from Air Fleet Five in Scandinavia were reinforcing Air Fleet Two in France.

The signs were ominous. British military chiefs had studied aerial photographs taken by high-flying, camouflaged Spitfires, and realized that an invasion was imminent. Since the Channel tides at the moment favoured an attacking force, they came to the conclusion that the Germans would probably invade within the next few days.

On the night of 6th September, R.A.F. Blenheims were sent to bomb the invasion ports. The British

Opposite A spotter on the roof-tops of London scans the sky for enemy aircraft.

Home Fleet at Scapa Flow in Scotland was ordered to stand-by in readiness to sail south.

The Government was informed "attack probable within next three days" and, on 7th September, the Air Ministry signalled Dowding "landing considered imminent."

On the evening of 7th September, the military chiefs decided that forward divisions along the south and east coasts of England should be geared to a high state of readiness. They therefore signalled to Eastern and Southern Commands the code-word "Cromwell," which meant "invasion imminent."

Some of the Home Guard commanders, acting on their own initiative and influenced by the savage air attacks on London, thought that the invasion would come that night, and decided actually to call out their men.

Throughout towns and villages in southern England, the church bells began to ring again – the warning signal that the Germans were coming. Home Guards made tearful farewells to wives and families, and went off to spend an all-night vigil waiting for invaders who would never come.

Some bridges were destroyed; tank traps were set up, and troops stood by on the roads leading to Canterbury, Maidstone and Horsham. Rumours soon spread of enemy parachutist landings, and of German E-boats approaching the coast.

As Churchill said later, although it was a false alarm, it "served as a useful tonic and rehearsal for all concerned."

A member of the Auxiliary Fire Service (do you see the A.F.S. on his helmet?) calls out directions to the squad below him.

A London scene

On 7th September and the nights that followed, German bombs fell mainly on the docks of West Ham and Bermondsey, the factories and gasworks of Poplar, on Shoreditch, Whitechapel and Stepney, where thousands of people were crowded together, up to twelve in a house.

That first night alone, 430 people were killed and 1,600 seriously injured, while thousands more were made homeless. Fires spread from West Ham to Tower Bridge, amidst heaps of rubble and fallen masonry. St. Paul's Cathedral stood out against a "sky of khaki."

"The scene was like a lake in hell," a Thames patrolman at Woolwich said. "Burning barges drifting everywhere."

At the Surrey docks, where 250 acres of timber was ablaze, a fire officer urgently demanded: "Send all the bloody pumps you've got; the whole bloody world's on fire." Many firemen were cut off and perished in the flames.

The following day, a Sunday, had been chosen some time before as a national day of prayer. There was little time for prayer in the East End, scene of the worst devastation.

An American journalist described London's streets as being "full of rubble blown up from direct hits, filled with glass, brick, furniture and plaster. Water mains were smashed right and left."

Three main railway stations had been badly damaged, and all rail traffic running in and out of London from the south came to a halt. But, in the West End, theatres and cinemas were full, and the streets were crowded with casual traffic.

Unexploded bombs, known as U.X.B.s, made the rescue and clearance work a nightmare. Some of

A warehouse beside the Thames lit up by the fire raging inside (September 1940).

Winston Churchill and his
wife inspect bomb damage
in the City of London after
a particularly bad raid.

them might be duds, and quite harmless; but others
could have delayed action fuses, and explode suddenly,
without warning.

Bomb disposal squads worked heroically to dismantle these U.X.B.s. One bomb, which had fallen
close to St. Paul's Cathedral, took three days to be
extricated by two army engineers. Then it was
driven at high speed through the East End to Hackney
Marshes, where it was blown up, making a hole
100 feet in diameter. King George VI had just
instituted a new medal for bravery, the George
Cross. The two engineers, Lieutenant Davies and
Sapper Wylie, were to become the first two holders
of the award.

On 13th September, a German raider attacked
Buckingham Palace. The Queen remarked: "I'm
glad we've been bombed. It makes me feel I can look
the East End in the face."

Ack-ack guns and barrage balloons

Since there were not many suitable night fighter aircraft, the defence of London and other major cities against nocturnal air raids depended largely on anti-aircraft guns and searchlights. When London was first attacked by night, the defence was very poor, and many Londoners angrily demanded: "What happened to the guns?"

But anti-aircraft, or ack-ack guns, were also in short supply. There were in fact only a mere two thousand of them, instead of the eight thousand thought necessary to protect the country. And most of these were guarding aircraft factories and other military installations. Furthermore, the guns used were mostly too old-fashioned to deal with fast, high-flying aircraft. The searchlight situation was slightly better – there were four thousand of them available.

Within two days, however, Lieutenant General Frederick Pile, chief of Anti-Aircraft Command, had managed to double the number of guns around London. He also ordered each gun to fire as it pleased, in a mighty "barrage."

And so, when the Germans next came over, on the night of 10th September, five hundred guns opened up together. The noise was frightful. The guns did

A barrage balloon floats above the House of Commons. However, it didn't stop the German bombers getting through and bombing Parliament.

not inflict much damage, but they added to the strain on the attackers, and forced them to fly higher. And the Londoners loved it. At last, they thought, something positive was being done to hit back at the enemy.

But, without radar equipment to tackle the unseen raiders, the guns and searchlights could achieve little. They still relied on sound locators, which only picked up the sound waves from the bombers once they were well overhead. And the searchlight beams could not illuminate above 12,000 feet, while the raiders usually flew considerably higher than that.

The chance of a direct hit was therefore remote. The gunners, as in duck-shooting, had to estimate the aircraft's speed, fire ahead of the intended victim, and hope for the best.

The sky above London and many other cities was filled with hundreds of barrage balloons, like "herds of elephants," which were used to discourage dive-bombing and low-level attacks. As many as 1,500 might be herded together at a height of 5,000 feet. The largest and most crumpled balloon over London was called "Hermann."

These balloons were operated by crews from R.A.F. Balloon Command, and were wound up and down from sites in parks and open spaces.

Opposite An anti-aircraft (or ack-ack) battery on the south coast of England.

Left A German Dornier plunges down into the English Channel.

Drama in the sky

Every day brought its share of drama and of heroes. Pilots on both sides fought heroically, but also humanely – only occasionally did hatred and anger get the better of men.

Flight Lieutenant James Nicholson, a gangling, mop-headed, toothy 23 year-old was lucky not to have been killed by mistake. He was flying at 17,000 feet over Hampshire when his Hurricane was set ablaze during a fight with Messerschmitts. Nicholson continued fighting but at last baled out, dropping 5,000 feet sheer before his burned hands could manage to pull the parachute rip-cord. As he floated down, shots were fired at him and he was wounded. A Home Guard had mistaken the pilot for a German! For his ordeal, Nicholson was to be the first and only

Fighter Command pilot to be awarded the Victoria
Cross.

Perhaps the luckiest man to survive the battle
was Spitfire pilot Flight Lieutenant Alan Deere, a
rugged 21 year-old New Zealander. Deere had
already survived a Dunkirk bale-out and two forced
landings, when he tried to bale-out again and found
that his parachute was fouled up in the cockpit. He
just managed to get clear before the plane crashed,
and, on landing, he was given a lift by a passing
ambulance. Two weeks later, Deere landed in the
middle of a plum tree near a Kent farmhouse. The
farmer, shotgun in hand, demanded: "Did you have
to land in my best plum tree?"

Three days later, Deere's Spitfire was bombed on
take-off. It was blown into the air by the blast, sucked
down again and skidded upside down for a hundred
yards. Deere was not badly injured, and was soon
back in action.

In his first combat, Sergeant Ray Holmes shot
down two German Dorniers before colliding with
another one over London. Holmes baled out, landed
on a rooftop and finished up in a dustbin. The
Dornier crashed into Victoria Station.

Another Sergeant, 23 year-old Ronnie Hamlyn,
veteran of Dunkirk, was on a charge of negligence
the day his squadron was scrambled three times. As
the pilot touched down for the third time, his com-
mading officer said: "As it seems impossible to meet
you in my office, Hamlyn, I hereby officially
admonish you." Hamlyn, who that day had shot
down a record five victims, was also officially
commended – he was awarded the Distinguished
Flying Medal.

Battle control

Thanks to the foresight of Air Chief Marshal Dowding, Fighter Command possessed an unrivalled defence system, with a complex yet simple network of control and communications to aid interception of enemy aircraft.

As soon as the radar screen detected enemy raiders approaching the British coast, constantly manned telephone lines began to hum as the raiders' position, height and numbers were passed direct to Fighter Command Headquarters at Stanmore in Middlesex.

This information would be processed, or filtered, in the Command Filter Room. W.A.A.F. plotters, with croupier sticks, would push counters representing the enemy aircraft across a large table map and soon built up an overall picture of enemy activity. The state of readiness of each squadron was displayed on another large board.

Then the filtered information, or plots, was passed to one or more of the four group headquarters, which would decide which sector station should deal with the enemy.

Finally, the sector station would scramble the required number of squadrons which, once airborne, would be given the latest information by radio-telephone.

Thus the R.A.F. fighters could be directed to the exact correct position to intercept the enemy, instead of having to waste precious time and fuel searching him out.

Once the filtering had been done, Dowding left the operational control of the battle to his group commanders.

No. 11 Group, whose fighters bore the brunt of the battle over south-east England, was the most hard-pressed group. Its underground headquarters

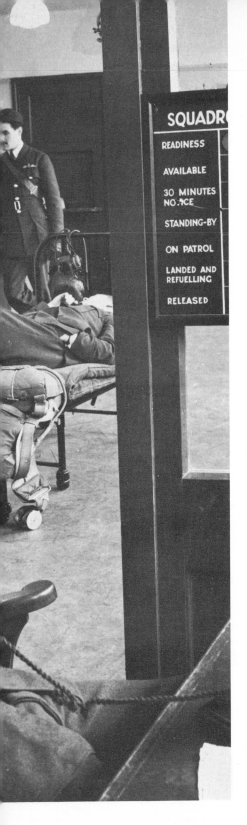

SQUADR[O]

READINESS

AVAILABLE

30 MINUTES NO[T]ICE

STANDING-BY

ON PATROL

LANDED AND REFUELLING

RELEASED

Call for action: enemy aircraft have been spotted crossing the Channel. The control room receives the information, and scrambles the necessary squadrons.

at Uxbridge, known as "The Hole", was daily the scene of feverish activity as R.A.F. officers and W.A.A.F.s sifted incoming reports and controlled the squadrons in the air and on the ground.

After the German raiders had passed through the radar screen, the task of tracking the enemy was taken over by the Royal Observer Corps. Churchill called this "a transition from the middle of the twentieth century to the early Stone Age."

The Corps of 30,000 men had 1,500 observation posts strung out on hilltops and other vantage points. Each post was manned by two men – one with an optical device to plot the raiders, the other with a telephone to pass on the information.

The network of communications between radar stations, observer posts, operations rooms and airfields was maintained throughout the battle by the untiring efforts of Post Office workers.

5. The few triumph

On 11th September, Winston Churchill warned the British nation: "If this invasion is to be tried at all, it does not seem that it can be long delayed."

Were the Germans coming at last? Adolf Hitler was still waiting for Germany to gain air supremacy but he was sure that, given one more spell of good weather, the Luftwaffe would finally succeed in destroying the Royal Air Force.

Reich Marshal Goering, as cocksure as ever, was convinced that his Luftwaffe was almost within reach of victory. On the few fine days during the last week when his bombers had been able to raid London and other targets, R.A.F. opposition had been surprisingly weak.

Goering was confident that one final onslaught was all that was needed to win the battle. On the next fine day, his aircraft would make a large-scale daylight raid on London, bomb the Londoners into submission and finish off the last of the R.A.F. fighters.

The big day, the most decisive day of the whole battle, was to be on Sunday, 15th September.

While aircraft of Field Marshal Kesselring's Air Fleet Two prepared to attack, Winston Churchill and his wife decided to visit Air Vice Marshal Keith Park at No. 11 Group headquarters in Uxbridge. It was a lovely sunny morning.

Escorting his two distinguished visitors down into "The Hole", Air Vice Marshal Park commented: "I don't know whether anything will happen today. At present all is quiet."

But Churchill was not to be denied his moment of history.

Below Inside a German 'plane the crew get ready to shoot down an attacking Spitfire.

Battle of Britain Day

Soon after 10 o'clock on the morning of Sunday, 15th September, the most momentous day of the whole battle, British radar picked up a large enemy force heading across the Channel.

The force of one hundred bombers and four hundred fighters from Air Fleet Two made a slow, ponderous crossing. In the meantime, Air Vice Marshal Park was able to put into the air eleven of his twenty-one squadrons, and, to the rear of London, a great wing of sixty fighters from No. 12 Group.

As the raiders crossed the Kent coast near Dover, R.A.F. fighters pierced the protective screen of escorts and, like a pack of hungry dogs, tore into the lumbering bombers.

Soon the German formations were broken up and many were shot down in flames. Others, however, struggled on to their objective, and disgorged their lethal loads on London. But then, to the dismay of the German aircrews, the wing of sixty fighters, led by legless pilot Douglas Bader, swept down from East Anglia, burst onto the scene and chased the enemy off.

The Luftwaffe returned again early that afternoon, but the R.A.F. pilots had had time to refuel and rearm.

Kesselring sent an advanced guard of almost two hundred fighters to sweep the skies clear of Spitfires and Hurricanes, and it was then that the long awaited all-out fighter battle took place.

Some fifteen British squadrons engaged the enemy and soon more than two hundred individual combats had broken out. "So crowded was the sky, it was like Piccadilly Circus in rush hour," said one pilot. In a tremendous fight, the R.A.F. remained unvanquished.

Above Hurricanes flying above the low-lying cloud. Notice the wing of the 'plane in which the photographer sat.

Opposite The legless air-ace, Douglas Bader, climbs into his cockpit for a thanksgiving flight over London, 1945.

The gathering clouds gave cover to the subsequent wave of German bombers, and many of them got through to London and dropped their bombs. But Bader's wing was soon in amongst them again, and the raiders were severely punished.

Britain claimed to have knocked out 185 German aircraft that day, for the loss of only twenty-eight R.A.F. fighters. In fact, no more than sixty enemy planes had actually been destroyed, although many others were damaged and their crews shot up.

Nevertheless, it was a great victory, and in future no more aerial armadas would be sent against Britain by day. Although it was not known then, this proved later to be the turning point of the whole battle, and was to lead Hitler to cancel his invasion plans.

Ever since, 15th September has been celebrated annually as "Battle of Britain Day," in memory of the "few."

Invasion postponed

In the meantime, Britain had been attacking Germany's invasion fleet with increasing intensity; naval forces and R.A.F. bombers severely bombarded the main Channel invasion ports of Ostend in Belgium, and Calais, Boulogne and Cherbourg in France.

Hitler, who had already delayed his decision to launch Operation Sea Lion, insisted again on the necessity of absolute command of the air.

On 14th September, he was warned by his naval staff: "The situation in the air does not at present permit the operation to be staged when account is taken of the grave risks involved." Hitler, therefore, decided to postpone the decision yet again. He would make up his mind on 17th September. This meant that, allowing ten days for the final preparations to be made, the invasion could not now take place before 27th September.

Even after the hammering the Luftwaffe had received on 15th September, Goering was still optimistic. "Four or five days of good weather and the R.A.F. will have lost all its fighters," he kept repeating.

But no-one else now shared the Reich Marshal's optimism, least of all his fighter pilots and bomber crews, who had been continually told that the R.A.F. had only a few aircraft left, only to find the British skies still thick with fighters.

Hitler's naval staff continued to report more and more sinkings among the invasion fleet, and Hitler was forced to agree with them when they pointed out that the R.A.F. was "still by no means defeated."

Furthermore, a period of rough weather was expected in the Channel instead of the flat calm necessary for the successful landing of a large force. On 17th September, Hitler ordered the postponement of Operation Sea Lion "until further notice."

Then, on 19th September, he ordered that no more shipping was to be assembled at Channel ports, and that shipping already there should be dispersed "in order to minimize the damage suffered in the course of enemy air attacks." By now, the British had sunk or damaged ten per cent of the total invasion fleet – 21 out of 170 transports, and 214 out of 1,918 barges.

The pretence of invasion was still kept up until 12th October, when Hitler formally admitted failure and called off his invasion until the following spring. But, by then, Hitler's thoughts had already turned towards another, bigger prey – Russia.

Opposite The end of a raid. A German 'plane brought down on the English coast during an air attack intended as a preliminary to Hitler's invasion.

Some British aces

WING COMMANDER DOUGLAS BADER Became a legend in his own life-time. Dashing young airman, brilliant rugby player and cricketer whose life seemed shattered when he lost both legs in an aircraft accident. Courageously rejoined the R.A.F. to help save his country, flying and fighting with artificial legs. An outspoken, domineering character, who would never take no for an answer. Given command of a Canadian Spitfire squadron and then led a wing of sixty fighters. An outstanding leader. Aged 30.

SQUADRON LEADER ADOLPH "SAILOR" MALAN A quiet-spoken, unflappable 30 year-old South African, who was an officer with the Union Castle shipping line before joining the R.A.F. in 1936. One of the R.A.F.'s greatest aces and tacticians. First saw action at Dunkirk, where he shot down five enemy planes and was awarded the D.F.C. Became commander of a Spitfire squadron and later saw intensive action at Biggin Hill. Was decorated for "commanding his squadron with outstanding success."

Some German aces

KOMMODOR ADOLF GALLAND Perhaps the Luftwaffe's greatest fighter ace. A flamboyant, good-looking, moody 28 year-old, who had always loved flying. Commanded respect of the men in his group; in combat was not easy to keep up with. Off-duty he enjoyed the company of the high-living Berlin movie crowd, fast cars, gambling, girls. Smoked cigars while flying, and had a setter dog called Pig's Belly. Along with Molders, was the most decorated Luftwaffe pilot. By the end of 1940, had 57 "kills."

KOMMODOR WERNER MOLDERS This slim, intelligent 26 year-old was a great fighter ace and accomplished tactician. Was Germany's top scorer in the Spanish Civil War and had destroyed twenty-five enemy planes by 1940. A calm disciplined leader. Like Galland, voiced his opinion of Goering and the Luftwaffe's administration in general. A devout Catholic.

The blitz

Although his invasion plans had been thwarted, Hitler was by no means finished with Britain, nor especially with London. From 7th September to 3rd November, London's seven million inhabitants were "blitzed" for fifty-seven consecutive nights by an average of 160 bombers, dropping on average two hundred tons of bombs and nearly two hundred canisters of incendiaries each night.

While a million shelters had been provided, every night thousands of weary people sought refuge in the underground, under railway arches, in slit trenches. At one time, 177,000 people were sleeping in seventy-nine tube stations, where the sanitation and washing facilities were appalling.

Fires raged everywhere, and were often so huge that the fire-fighters were quite helpless, "like little boys peeing on an enormous bonfire." Nevertheless, thousands of fires were put out before they had taken hold by an army of vigilant fire-watchers.

Before a raid, sirens would give a two-minute "warbling" noise and dogs would howl, until the roar of guns was mingled with the sound of falling bombs and clattering incendiaries, to be followed by the thud of collapsing walls. A steady siren blast would give the all-clear.

Above After a raid during the blitz, an injured person is carried to an ambulance by a team of rescuers; notice their tin helmets, and the rope to hold back sightseers.

Hollow-eyed air raid wardens would be everywhere; civil defence teams would drag dead and wounded alike from the rubble, white with dust and streaked with blood; first aid was dispensed from small improvised posts, a multitude of which had sprung up to relieve the hospitals, which were already overcrowded with mutilated people; food would simmer over makeshift field-kitchens.

Time and time again, drains were smashed, and light, power and gas supplies cut off. Traffic would come to a standstill, and most railways became paralyzed.

The comic and bizarre went hand in hand – a lady hurled out into the street in her bath; corpses from Madame Tussaud's waxworks littering the street; old ladies crawling out of bomb ruins and calling for a bottle of beer.

There were more raids that winter, and the blitz did not finally end until 10th May, 1941 – the last and worst night of all. During the blitz, nearly 20,000 Londoners were to die and 1,400,000, or one Londoner in every six, made homeless.

But life and work went on. Shops, with signs like "More Open Than Usual" and "Blast!" became symbols of defiance. "See yer in the morning, boys" became a war-cry, as the Cockney people proved that "London can take it."

These firemen are clearing up in a damaged warehouse. See how the bomb blast has shattered all the windows. Warehouses were particularly vulnerable to bomb attacks, since they were large targets, and the goods stored in them burned easily.

Raids on provincial cities

Despite the severe mauling the Luftwaffe had received, Goering persisted in daylight raids over Britain, although on a much reduced scale, which caused tremendous damage to aircraft factories in the Southampton and Bristol areas.

Then Goering switched to sneak raids by high-flying fighter-bombers in an attempt to beat the British defences. But losses continued without the desired results.

Daylight raids gradually fizzled out altogether, and 31st October, 1940, is the official date for the end of the Battle of Britain. Yet that winter was to be the worst in British history, as German bombers roamed at night almost totally unopposed over the whole country.

Early in November, Goering ordered that the air offensive was to be entirely concentrated on night bombing, with industrial centres and ports as chief targets.

The new offensive was launched with an attack against Coventry on the night of 14th November. Helped by a full moon (known as "bombers' moon"), and a special Pathfinder force which dropped incendiaries to start fires to guide them, the bombers had no difficulty in dropping their loads right on target.

For ten hours, five hundred bombers in wave after wave dropped six hundred tons of high explosives and thousands of incendiaries on Coventry alone. A hundred acres in the centre of the city was left a smoking, crumbling pile of rubble, the medieval cathedral was in ruins, and 554 people were killed and 865 seriously injured.

About one third of the city's houses were damaged, not a single railway line was usable, over half the buses were wrecked and six out of seven telephone lines were cut. In addition, twenty-one important factories, including twelve directly concerned with aircraft manufacture, were badly wrecked. The Germans boasted that the city had been "Coventrated."

The next city to be "Coventrated" was Birmingham, which suffered greatly in three successive raids from 19th to 22nd November, with 800 people killed and 2,000 injured.

Southampton was heavily bombed on 24th November, and its city centre was devastated a week later. On 25th November, it was Bristol's turn. "We've been through hell," a Bristol woman wrote in her diary. "Never have I experienced anything like it. Tummy still wobbly."

By the end of the year, other provincial cities and ports including Manchester, Sheffield, Leicester, Liverpool, Portsmouth, Plymouth, Leeds and Glasgow had all suffered from the night raiders.

The tower of Coventry Cathedral stands alone among the ruins of the city, the result of one night's terrible bombing (14th November 1940).

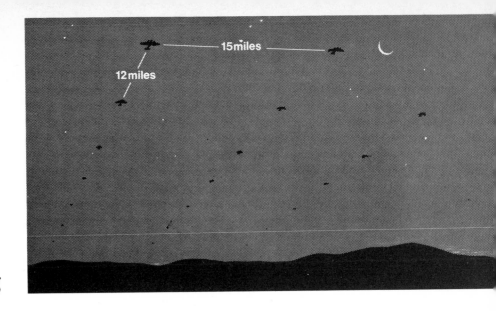

15miles

12miles

Night flying

"How can this happen?" the British public was asking. "How can German bombers enjoy such freedom of our skies at night when they were so soundly thrashed by the R.A.F. during the day?"

The truth was that night fighting was still very much in its infancy. Britain did not yet have the answer to counter these high-flying nocturnal bombing raids. Fighters and anti-aircraft guns were just not as efficient as they were during the day.

The chief thing they lacked was proper radar equipment – to track the raiders overland (since ground observers were "blind" at night); to help fighters intercept and shoot down the enemy; and to enable the guns to fire accurately at unseen targets.

Until radar was made widely available to provide the necessary information, the defenders could achieve very little. That winter Britain had fewer than twelve squadrons of night fighters, and only two of these flew modern aircraft equipped with up-to-date radar equipment. The ack-ack guns guarding the cities did their best but, without proper radar guidance, they could inflict very few casualties on the raiders.

The Germans made interception as difficult as possible by flying in "crocodile" formation. Bombers

would fly singly one behind the other at intervals of
twelve miles and in several lines fifteen miles apart.
With only one raider per 180 square miles, inter-
cepting was just like looking for the proverbial
needle in a haystack.

One problem the Germans did have was navigation – they found it hard to make their way to a
given target in the dark. A system, called *Knickebein,*
had been developed: two radio stations on the
Continent would send radio beams, like invisible
searchlights, so arranged that they would cross over
any target in Britain. An aircraft would fly along one
beam until the second one was detected, and would
then drop its bombs.

But the British found out about *Knickebein* and
were able to jam or deflect the beams. This caused
the bombers to wander around aimlessly, or go
completely astray.

The Germans then adopted a new device, called
"X apparatus," a different form of radio guide. This
was used by a Pathfinder force of fighter-bombers
which, once having located the target, dropped
incendiary bombs to start fires as a guide to the
bombers following behind. This technique was first
used in the raid on Coventry.

Below Checking the course:
fighter pilots having a last
look at the map before
taking off on a night
mission.

The final reckoning

Until the British Government rejected his peace offers and came out in open defiance, Hitler had had no thoughts of conquering Britain. He had always counted on British commonsense to see the hopelessness of the situation and so accept his peace terms.

When his seaborne invasion plans were thwarted by the R.A.F., and night-bombing was unable to break the British spirit or sufficiently interrupt her war production, Hitler's thoughts turned eastwards.

This was nothing new. For some time, Hitler had been thinking about the conquest of Russia, not just for personal ambition, but because he hated Communism. As British resistance persisted, so these thoughts became more attractive.

Hitler's invasion of Russia which began on 22nd June, 1941, granted Britain a much-needed reprieve. It also left the country as a perpetual thorn in Hitler's side, and as a base from which forces would eventually be sent for the final overthrow of Nazi Germany.

Hitler missed his best chance of invasion when Britain lay practically defenceless in July, 1940, after the collapse of France. As the months slipped by, so did Hitler's chances of success.

If Operation Sea Lion had succeeded, the Nazi occupation of Britain would not have been pleasant. Orders had been given to the invasion armies to arrest all able-bodied males between the ages of 17 and 45, and send them to prison camps on the Continent.

Britain would also have been systematically plundered, and her remaining inhabitants terrorized. "Trouble-makers" would have been dealt with by the secret police, under Professor Franz Six, who was later responsible for wholesale massacres in Russia.

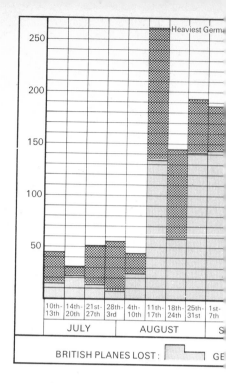

The numbers of aircraft lost respectively by the British and the Germans.

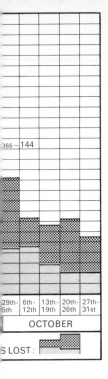

oss – 144

29th-5th	6th-12th	13th-19th	20th-26th	27th-31st

OCTOBER

S LOST :

The Battle of Britain, which saved the nation from this fate, officially lasted from 10th July to 31st October, 1940. During that period, the Luftwaffe lost 1,733 aircraft while the R.A.F. had 915 fighters destroyed. At the time, the British claimed to have destroyed 2,698 aircraft, and the Germans 3,058.

The Luftwaffe might in fact have succeeded in knocking out Fighter Command, had not Goering changed tactics so often. The Luftwaffe also lacked the one weapon necessary for success – the four-engine heavy bomber.

In the final analysis, however, it was the small, young band of R.A.F. fighter pilots who, inspired by Churchill and controlled by Dowding, won the battle by their skill and bravery. Theirs was the supreme triumph.

It was fighter pilots like these, ready at a moment's notice to take off and defend England against the German air attacks, who really won the Battle of Britain, and prevented Hitler's invasion of the British Isles.

Table of Dates

1935

July	First British radar stations built.
6th November	Maiden flight of the first Hurricane.

1936

5th March	First Spitfire flight.
14th July	Air Chief Marshal Dowding is appointed Commander-in-Chief of Fighter Command.

1939

May and August	*Graf Zeppelin* spies on British radar stations.
3rd September	Germany invades Poland. Start of World War Two.

1940

10th May	Churchill forms a new British government.
10th June	Italy declares war.
14th June	German troops enter Paris.
18th June	"I expect the Battle of Britain is about to begin" – Churchill speech.
2nd July	Hitler orders preliminary invasion study.
10th July	Official beginning of the Battle of Britain. A convoy off Dover is attacked.
16th July	Hitler orders preparation of the invasion, to be called Operation Sea Lion.
25th July	A convoy is attacked in the Channel; eight ships are sunk, and three damaged.
1st August	Hitler directs the Luftwaffe to destroy the R.A.F.
8th August	A Channel convoy is attacked, seven ships lost and many more damaged.
12th August	Luftwaffe attacks against radar stations and airfields.
13th August	Eagle Day – the Luftwaffe launch their big assault.
15th August	Black Thursday – the Luftwaffe's worst day. Air Fleet Five is knocked out of the battle.

20th August	Churchill makes a speech praising "the few."
24th August	London is accidentally bombed during Goering's second bid for air supremacy.
25th August	The R.A.F. bomb Berlin.
30th–31st August	The worst week-end for the R.A.F.
2nd September	Hitler orders raids on British cities as reprisal for the bombing of Berlin.
6th September	The R.A.F. bomb the Channel invasion ports.
7th September	Mass daylight bombing of London. Invasion false alarm.
	First of fifty-seven consecutive nights of bombing on London.
10th September	Hitler postpones invasion decision until 14th September.
11th September	Churchill warns the nation that an invasion seems imminent.
14th September	Hitler delays invasion decision until 17th September.
15th September	Battle of Britain Day, which marks a turning point in the battle.
17th September	Hitler postpones Operation Sea Lion until further notice.
19th September	Hitler orders the dispersal of the invasion fleet.
12th October	Hitler puts off the invasion until the following spring.
31st October	Official end of the Battle of Britain.
Early November	Goering concentrates entirely on night-bombing.
14th November	Coventry heavily bombed.
25th November	Bristol bombed.
	Air Chief Marshal Dowding retires.
1941	
10th May	London's last and worst night of the blitz.
22nd June	Hitler invades Russia.

Glossary

AIRSHIP A cigar-shaped balloon filled with gas and powered by a motor and propeller.

APPEASEMENT The attempt to conciliate an enemy by making concessions. The word is often used in connexion with the British government's policy towards Nazi Germany in the 1930s.

BARRAGE BALLOON A balloon made of rubber-proofed cotton, filled with hydrogen. It was supposed to obstruct enemy aircraft.

BLITZ A colloquial term for an intensive air attack, abbreviated from the German *Blitzkrieg*.

BLITZKRIEG German word meaning lightning war. Mobile warfare by combined armoured and air forces, which was first used by the Nazis against Poland in 1939.

CANNIBALIZE Strip down old or broken machines to provide spare parts.

CATHODE RAY TUBE A vacuum tube used in radar to measure the length of the pulse from the transmitter to the aircraft and back again.

DIVE BRAKES These brakes allowed Stukas to dive nearly vertically at carefully controlled speeds. This gave them very great bombing accuracy.

HOME GUARD An unpaid force who were supposed to protect the country in case of invasion.

INCENDIARY BOMBS Bombs filled with inflammable material which were dropped in order to start fires.

NAZI General term for Hitler's fascist party (National Socialist German Workers' Party).

PANZER A German word meaning armour, and used to describe regiments which included tanks or armoured vehicles.

PATHFINDER An aircraft sent ahead of a group of bombers to guide them to their target.

PILLBOX A small round concrete fort, built mainly underground, as a protection against air attacks.

PLOTTER The person who calculates the movements of aircraft, and marks them up on charts.

PROPAGANDA Biased information designed to convert people to a particular point of view.

PROTOTYPE The first example of a machine from which other models are developed.

RADAR A system for judging the direction and distance of aircraft and other objects, by measuring the radio waves which they reflect.

RECEIVER The directional aerial used in radar to pick up the echo from approaching aircraft.

SCHWÄRME A group of four German fighters, flying in pairs.

SCRAMBLE Take off (as applied to aircraft).

SECTOR STATION The main R.A.F. fighter station in a particular area, or sector.

SORTIE An aircraft's operational flight.

SOUND LOCATOR A device for determining the direction of sound waves.

SPOTTER PLANE An aircraft which makes aerial surveys, for example to spot a crashed aircrew in the sea.

SQUADRON A unit in the R.A.F., consisting usually of about twelve aircraft.

STUKA An abbreviation for the German word *Sturzkampfflugzeug*, meaning dive-bomber.

TRANSMITTER The directional aerial used in radar to transmit radio waves.

VAPOUR TRAIL A trail of gaseous smoke given out by aircraft engines.

VERY PISTOL A pistol which fires a coloured flare used as a signal.

W.A.A.F. Women's Auxiliary Air Force, now known as the Women's Royal Air Force (W.R.A.F.).

WEAVERS Aircraft which fly backwards and forwards to guard other planes.

WING An R.A.F. unit of three or more squadrons.

Further Reading

Bickers, R. T., *Ginger Lacey, Fighter Pilot* (Pan, 1969).

Bishop, Edward, *Their Finest Hour* (Macdonald, 1969).

Brickhill, Paul, *Reach for the Sky* – the story of Douglas Bader (Fontana, 1969).

Collier, Basil, *The Battle of Britain* (Fontana, 1969).

Collier, Richard, *Eagle Day* (Pan, 1968).

Deere, Alan, *Nine Lives* (Hodder & Stoughton, 1969).

Fitzgibbon, Constantine, *Blitz* (Macdonald, 1970).

Galland, Adolf, *The First and the Last* (Methuen, 1970).

Hillary, Richard, *The Last Enemy* (Pan, 1969).

Johnson, J. Edgar, *Full Circle* – the story of air fighting (Pan, 1969).

Jullian, Marcel, *The Battle of Britain* (Panther, 1969).

Killen, John, *The Luftwaffe* (Sphere, 1969).

Price, Alfred, *The Luftwaffe* (Macdonald, 1970).

Townsend, Peter, *Duel of Eagles* (Weidenfeld & Nicholson, 1970).

Wallace, Graham, *R.A.F. Biggin Hill* (Tandem, 1969).

Wright, Robert, *Dowding and the Battle of Britain* (Corgi, 1970).

Index

Picture Credits

The author and publishers wish to thank all those who have given
permission to reproduce copyright illustrations on the following pages:
Camera Press, 16 (top); Central Press Photos, 22–23; Conway
Picture Library, *frontispiece, jacket* (back), 16 (bottom), 18, 26, 32–33,
35, 39, 43, 47, 50–51, 52–53, 54–55, 62–63, 64, 65, 70–71, 72–73, 78,
87, 89; Imperial War Museum, 12, 16 (centre), 40, 42, 59, 76–77,
80 (top); Keystone, 8, 11, 16 (top), 17, 25, 31, 36, 48–49, 56, 80
(bottom), 81, 82–83; Paul Popper, 77; Radio Times Hulton Picture
Library, 14, 17 (centre), 22 (top), 24, 29, 30, 34, 44–45, 48, 51, 56–57,
60, 61, 66, 67, 68, 69, 70, 74, 75, 82, 85; United Artists Corporation,
jacket (front and flaps).

The maps and drawings were done by Grout, Fry and Associates.